The Heavenly Connection

*Reaching
Spiritual Maturity*

Lila B. Mullins

TO
those who have
urged and encouraged me to
continue my writing

TO
those who have
stated that my words have
made a difference in their
lives

TO
JOEY BINKLEY
a wise and faithful woman
whose support and inspiration
have made my efforts worthwhile

THE HEAVENLY CONNECTION

Do not cast me away when I am old;
do not forsake me when my strength
is gone

Even when I am old and gray, do not
forsake me, O God, till I declare
your power to the next generation,
your might to all who are to come.

—Psalm 71:9, 18

Contents

ISBN: 0-9650991-1-3

Additional copies may be ordered from your local bookstore or:

Librom Publishing
2809 12th Avenue South
Nashville, TN 37204

PREFACE

If I recall my childhood days accurately almost all stories began, "Once upon a time." As soon as my mother read these words my excitement heightened, and even after I learned to read, those first words still brought a feeling of anticipation, enthusiasm and exhilaration.

Can we, as adults, recapture the stimulation and anticipation of the words, "Once upon a time," as we read the most important book of all, the Holy Bible? I believe we can.

Once upon a time God created the heavens and the earth; once upon a time God created man from the dust of the ground and breathed into his nostrils life. Once upon a time there were men named Noah, Abraham, Moses, Jacob and Joseph. Each account of their lives is an exciting story.

Once upon a time there was a Gentile woman named Ruth from the land of Moab who became the great-grandmother of David. Once upon a time there was a Jewish girl named Esther who became the wife of Xerxes I, king of Persia. It is a story of intrigue, suspense and danger in the royal palace.

As we come to the New Testament there are many narratives that could begin with "Once upon a time." Once upon a time there was a young couple named Joseph and Mary who were engaged to be married. Before the wedding took place, Mary, who was a virgin, was visited by an angel announcing that she would be the mother of Jesus the Christ who would save people from their sins. Once upon a time in Bethlehem, the city of David, a baby was born—God in the flesh, who came down from heaven to this earth to be the Savior of mankind.

Once upon a time He was betrayed in a garden, judged unjustly before ruthless men and crucified on a cross to bear the sins of the whole world. His body was laid to rest in a cave—He rose victorious on the third day and returned to heaven to prepare a place for us so that in time our heavenly connection will be culminated in eternal life. Christ descended so that we can ascend.

As we begin the journey through this book, reaffirming our heavenly connection, may we again experience the thrill of "Once upon a time."

INTRODUCTION

From the time of our birth, even before, we have a heavenly connection. God created us in His own image and breathed into us the breath of life.

The Lord God formed the man from the dust of the ground and breathed into his nostrils the breath of life, and the man became a living being.

—Genesis 2:7

It is important for us to keep in mind how we were made. Job speaking to God reminds us:

Your hands shaped me and made me. . . .Remember that you molded me like clay.

—Job 10:8, 9

Another reminder is recorded in Psalm 103:14:

. . .for He knows how we are formed, He remembers that we are dust.

Isaiah remembered:

Yet, O Lord, you are our Father. We are the clay, You are the potter; we are all the work of your hand.

—Isaiah 64:8

But this is not the whole story. If clay was the only ingredient we would be like the lower animals, but because God loved the man He has made He gave him something special—too wonderful for us to comprehend—an eternal spirit.

Because we consist of two components, flesh and spirit, there is a constant conflict between the two. We call it spiritual warfare; a battle of good versus evil. The danger signals and warnings are revealed to us in the Bible and we must be on guard constantly and remain alert.

Watch and pray so that you will not fall into temptation. The spirit is willing, but the body is weak.

—Matthew 26:41

God knows that man's humanity is frail and weak and that we need strength to combat Satan and his angels of darkness.

> For Satan himself masquerades as an angel of light. It is not surprising then, if his servants masquerade as servants of righteousness. Their end will be what their actions deserve.
> —2 Corinthians 11:14, 15

We must do everything possible to equip ourselves so that we can adequately combat Satan and his evil forces. The battle is ongoing and we cannot become complacent and let down our guard.

The purpose of this book, hopefully, is to inspire and aid us on our pilgrim journey so that we can live productive lives in service to God and others with the hope and assurance that heaven will be our home when the battle is over and at last we can lay down our armor

JARS OF CLAY

For we do not preach ourselves, but Jesus Christ as Lord, and ourselves as your servants for Jesus' sake.

For God, who said, "Let light shine out of darkness," made his light shine in our hearts to give us the light of the knowledge of the glory of God in the face of Christ.

But we have this treasure in jars of clay to show that this all-surpassing power is from God and not from us.
—2 Corinthians 4:5-7

The oldest craft in Bible lands is pottery making. At first the clay was molded in the hand but later it was discovered it could be shaped by rotation in a circular hole in the ground. Wooden molds were also used. A very primitive potter's wheel may have been in use by 1900 B. C.

Many items were made from clay—oil lamps, bowls, pots for water and for cooking utensils, and also knives and combs. Special care was taken in making pots for water so they would not leak and an extra lump of clay was added on the bottom for strength.

Doves and pigeons found a use for clay pots when they made their nests in the ones on the flat roofs of the hillside houses of Nazareth.

Designs were scratched into the clay and sometimes decorative designs were discovered accidentally such as the rope design. When a rope was tied around a jar to hold it in place while drying a pretty design was imprinted as the rope was removed.

Scraps of clay were used to write letters and documents and to record family history. Broken pieces were used as ballots by voters.

Clay is pliable and the potter can change the shape and size as he turns the clay object. If the clay has hardened he can add water and continue to reshape.

Sometimes we forget that we are made of clay—the miry, muddy, earthy clay.

As a Father has compassion on his children, so the Lord has compassion on those who fear him; for he knows how we are formed, he remembers that we are dust.
—Psalm 103:13, 14

Elihu speaking to Job,

I am just like you before God; I too have been taken from clay.
—Job 33:6

Yet, O Lord, you are our Father. We are the clay, you are the potter;
we are all the work of your hand.
—Isaiah 64:8

Why did God form us from clay? Was there a special reason for choosing this particular element? Was marble too cold; gold dust too hard and unpliable; brass too shiny? Maybe it's because clay, in the hands of the potter, can be molded and reshaped continually.

If we get side-tracked along life's pathway, leave the course and head in the wrong direction, God can add a little water to the drying clay and remake us—that is, if we are willing to submit to Him.

Have Thine own way, Lord, have Thine
*   own way;*
Thou art the Potter, I am the clay!
Mold me and make me after Thy will
While I am waiting yielded and still.

This song goes back to my earliest remembrance but I confess that only in recent years has the true meaning made an impact on me. We never reach perfection but we strive towards it, and in the hands of the Master Craftsman we are daily being molded into His likeness.

God has given to us, jars of clay, the Great Commission. He has entrusted us, made of dust, to carry out His work.

Therefore go and make disciples of all nations, baptizing them in the
name of the Father and of the Son and of the Holy Spirit, and teach-
ing them to obey everything I have commanded you. And surely I
am with you always, to the very end of the age.
—Matthew 28:19, 20

He could have commissioned the angels to preach the good news of Christ or He could have created special beings for this purpose—but He chose us, dust in clay jars.

What a marvelous concept!

AMBASSADOR FOR THE KING

The word ambassador has an important sound, doesn't it? What does it mean? The dictionary gives a lengthy definition, but mainly; it means representative, delegate, chosen for a particular purpose.

When our government appoints ambassadors to other countries it appoints people of discretion and experienced in public relations. Representing the United States in a foreign country carries the responsibility of "selling" our nation in a favorable way.

Paul, even though in chains, said that he was an ambassador. Did he mean that he was an ambassador from one country to another? No—he was a delegated representative for Christ and no one has ever fought so tenaciously for the cause of Christ.

> *Pray also for me, that whenever I open my mouth, words may be given me so that I will fearlessly make known the mystery of the gospel, for which I am an ambassador in chains.*
> —Ephesians 6:19, 20

When you emerged from the waters of baptism to begin a new life you received the commission—ambassador for Christ Jesus, your Savior. You were delegated, appointed to tell others about the saving power of Christ.

> *Go into all the world and preach the good news to all creation.*
> —Mark 16:15

We dare not be hesitant or timid, but say as Paul,

> *I am not ashamed of the gospel, because it is the power of God for the salvation of everyone who believes.*
> —Romans 1:16

As full time ambassadors we must control our manner of life, not just on Sundays or certain times, but everywhere we go and whatever we do: in the classroom, in the office, in the market place, socially, on vacation and in the home.

It is necessary that our demeanor be in keeping with the Christian life. We must not be guilty of any behavior that would bring reproach on our Savior and the family of God.

Ours is a high calling and we want to be good representatives as we preach the good news of the gospel.

Isn't it wonderful to be an ambassador for the King?

All this is from God, who reconciled us to himself through Christ and gave us the ministry of reconciliation: that God was reconciling the world to himself in Christ, not counting men's sins against them. And he has committed to us the message of reconciliation. We are, therefore, Christ's ambassadors, as though God were making his appeal through us.

—2 Corinthians 5:18-20

FAITH'S YEAST

All of us have experienced the tantalizing aroma of freshly baked bread, either on entering a bakery or passing by. There is nothing quite like it. What makes this smell that causes our mouths to "water"?

Is it the flour? Is it the salt? Is it the liquid or the added vitamins? None of these. It is the leavening substance—yeast.

What does this have to do with faith? Let's find out. Yeast activates; sets the wheels in motion; causes the product to double in size, silently working its way into the other ingredients to complete the process—the end product—delicious bread.

Faith needs to be activated.

As the body without the spirit is dead, so faith without deeds is dead.
—James 2:26

If faith is stagnant—that is, only believing—it is unproductive and there are no results. Therefore, it is dead.

We have to prepare ourselves to be productive. The training begins with the Holy Word. As we read, study and meditate on the Scriptures, the desire to do good deeds naturally follows. We know that our deeds are not done to be noticed or draw attention to ourselves; neither are they done for "Brownie points" as if we have a list. Instead we quietly and unobtrusively go about serving others. Our salvation comes from God's grace through our faith and not from works performed or service rendered.

Be careful not to do your "acts of righteousness" before men to be seen by them. If you do, you will have no reward from your Father in heaven. So when you give to the needy, do not announce it with trumpets, as the hypocrites do in the synagogues and on the streets, to be honored by men. I tell you the truth, they have received their reward in full. But when you give to the needy, do not let your left hand know what your right hand is doing, so that your giving may be in secret. Then your Father, who sees what is done in secret, will reward you.

—Matthew 6:1-4

The yeast of faith is being compassionate, loving, understanding, encouraging, exhorting, forgetting self and serving others, producing fruits of the Spirit.

16

When we prepare ourselves for service, realizing our purpose for being, our good deeds will rise to the throne of Heaven, and God will be pleased and will reward us throughout eternity. In the meantime the yeast of our faith will ascend to our Father in a way similar to the aroma of freshly baked bread.

THE KEY

Do you realize the importance of keys? We have house keys and car keys; keys to deposit boxes and post office boxes. Have you ever lost your car keys or misplaced your house keys? It is a helpless and frustrating experience.

There are symbolic keys such as the key to the city given by a mayor to a person in recognition of service, or just as an honor. A young lady may wear a gold key on a chain given to her by her sweetheart signifying his love—the key to his heart.

There is another key that we have; that is, if we have heard the gospel call and obeyed. This key was given to us when we emerged from the waters of baptism and received the Holy Spirit. We may have overlooked this key from time to time. Due to neglect this key may be rusty or forgotten. It opens the door to God's prayer room and we need to use it regularly—in fact, daily.

God in His infinite wisdom made us creatures of choice; therefore we must take the initiative as no one else can unlock this door for us. God is waiting just inside but we have to unlock the door and enter.

Remember, there is no problem too small or too large that cannot be taken to the Lord in prayer. One of the greatest privileges we have as God's children is the advantage of prayer. If you have allowed your key to become rusty through neglect, resolve now to use it to unlock the door of prayer.

We may not always receive the answer we are looking for because God knows what is best for us. At other times our request may be delayed in order for us to become better prepared to receive what we have asked for.

We need to be patient and not expect immediate gratification.

Be still before the Lord and wait patiently for him.
—Psalm 37:7

I wait for the Lord, my soul waits, and in his word I put my hope.
—Psalm 130:5

In addition to prayer being a source of help in solving problems and requests for special favors, we must thank God for all He has done for us. Just as we thank people for kindness shown to us we must go to God in prayer and thank Him for his supreme love in the gift of His Son.

Prayer is also a time to praise, glorify and revere the Holy Name of God and our Savior. Thirty-six Psalms are devoted to expressions of joy and praise.

> *O Lord, our Lord, how majestic is your name in all the earth!*
> —Psalm 8:1

> *I will praise you, O Lord, with all my heart;*
> *I will tell of all your wonders.*
> *I will be glad and rejoice in you;*
> *I will sing praise to your name, O Most High.*
> —Psalm 9:1, 2

We also need to use prayer as a defense against the wiles of Satan. In Paul's letter to the Ephesians he gives instructions in regard to our battle against Satan's schemes. Prayer is a defense and will fortify us against evil.

The benefits of prayer are numerous and we short-change ourselves when we fail to take advantage of this avenue that leads to God's throne.

He is waiting for you! Unlock the door and enter God's prayer room today!

> *And pray in the Spirit on all occasions with all kinds of prayers and requests.*
> —Ephesians 6:18

> *The eyes of the Lord are on the righteous and his ears are attentive to their cry.*
> —Psalm 34:15

NIGHT SONG

The earth changes dramatically as the sun slowly sinks into oblivion and the daylight magically fades. Night approaches stealthily, wrapping the earth in a shroud of darkness that alters the countenance of the landscape.

Unlike the daylight with its gift of energy and activity, night brings a slowing down and a hushed atmosphere. There can be an ominous feeling associated with nightfall, especially for those of us who are older, alone and physically handicapped. We may be more apprehensive and fearful as the shades of night intensify and surround us.

At times sleep eludes us; pain escalates; our problems surface. Everyone, regardless of age, has been beset in the night by various things—pain, sorrow, tribulation. Have you ever heard someone say, "I thought the night would never end"?

How can we get through those long agonizing nights? Apparently Isaiah had nights of anguish as he cried,

My soul yearns for you in the night.

—Isaiah 26:9

David, as a result of sin and pursuit by enemies, was in turmoil and distress, but he beseeched the Lord and received an answer.

By day the Lord directs his love, at night his song is with me.
—Psalm 42:8

No night is too dark, no pain is so intense, no illness so serious, no sorrow so devastating, no tribulation so severe that cannot be more bearable when we take our burdens to God.

You will not fear the terror of night. . .nor the pestilence that stalks the darkness.
—Psalm 91:5, 6

Elihu knew that God gives songs in the night.

But no one says, "Where is God my Maker, who gives songs in the night."
—Job 35:10

God is with us in the blackest hour of the night; He has compassion and will give us His night song to comfort us if we ask. How
do I know? Because the Bible tells me so.

Surely he took up our infirmities and carried our sorrows.
—Isaiah 53:4

Let us then approach the throne of grace with confidence, so that we
may receive mercy and find grace to help us in our time of need.
—Hebrews 4:16

THE CENTERPIECE

I like to set a pretty table; in fact, I'm ALMOST more concerned about how the table looks than how the food tastes. The first thing of interest is the centerpiece. It may carry out a particular theme such as holidays, seasons, birthdays or weddings.

The centerpiece is the focal point and sets the tone and mood of the occasion. Most often it is made of flowers or fruit but other items can be incorporated in the design such as works of art, figurines or sculpture.

What is the centerpiece of your life? What is central in your thinking and foremost in your daily activities? Some may answer, "My family," others may say, "Education and career." These are important, of course.

Some people are workaholics to the extent that their jobs are all consuming and become the centerpiece of their lives. Another group says, "The church is the center of my life." This sounds good, doesn't it? But is this the right answer?

"Church work" can be very involved—committees of every kind, groups for different ages and interests; dinners, luncheons and showers. Then we have various ministries: singles, seniors, homeless, missionaries, prisoners. All of these things are good works and need to be done, but they must be placed in proper perspective to the centerpiece. In our concern for being involved in church work we may forget the real mission in our lives—to spread the good news of the gospel of Christ and to make sure that He is central to our lives.

> But God demonstrates his own love for us in this: While we were
> still sinners, Christ died for us.
> —Romans 5:8

Christ came into the world to save sinners (all of us). This is the message of the cross, that those who become baptized believers form the body of the church of which Christ is the head.

The transfiguration scene:

> Peter said to Jesus, "Lord, it is good for us to be here. If you wish, I
> will put up three shelters—one for you, one for Moses, and one for
> Elijah." While he was still speaking a bright cloud enveloped them,

and a voice from the cloud said, "This is my Son, whom I love; with
him I am well pleased. Listen to him!"

—Matthew 17:4, 5

The good deeds and other activities of the Christian life are the accessories to the centerpiece. Let's make sure we do not lose sight of the real focal point—Jesus the Christ, our Savior and King.

BORN TO DIE—TO LIVE AGAIN

What is the meaning of life? Do we give it much thought or are we too busy with the responsibilities and pressures of the here and now? It is easy to become earth bound—after all, this is all we know and have experienced.

James tells us in chapter 4, verse 14, "What is your life? You are a mist that appears for a little while and then vanishes." Our life could be compared to a cloud drifting across the morning sky; a shadow crossing in front of the moonlight—soon gone, like sand sifting through an hourglass.

God devised a magnificent plan in creating man in His own image, placing him on earth and sending him on a journey, pilgrims in an alien land. Life is a proving ground. Being human, we will make mistakes but these are not fatal and we are not out of the race; that is, if we are baptized believers in Christ Jesus and have accepted Him as our Savior. This entitles us to His mercy and grace if our penitence is genuine so that when we stumble and fall, miss the mark, leave the course, He is there to help us get back on track.

Life is also a warfare, a battle between the forces of good and evil, a conflict of the flesh and the spirit, a duel between the angels of darkness and the angels of light. We could call our life an overture or prelude to eternity. Even if we live threescore and ten or more years, our life span is no more than a wink of the eye or a flicker of a candle.

Life is a history lesson—God's wondrous story of mankind from the beginning. The Bible is so exciting as we read about the various peoples and nations in their struggles. The Word is so vividly written that we feel that we know these people and we can identify with their sins, trials and tribulations.

We feel sad when Abraham leaves his homeland to journey to unknown places and we are grieved as he and Isaac climb the mountain of Moriah. Then we rejoice as Abraham passes the test of faith.

The account of Moses and the Israelites is one of the most exciting in the Bible as they are enslaved by the Egyptians then led across the Red Sea on dry land on to the wilderness wanderings. We are in awe as we read of Joseph as he is sold by his jealous brothers, yet rises to power in Egypt in order to carry our God's purpose for his life.

Who can forget David, "a man after God's own heart"; yet he was guilty of dark and dastardly deeds? His life is an inspiration to us as we sin and fall, knowing if we are as truly repentant as David was, we, too, can be forgiven.

In the New Testament, we come to Peter as he denies the Lord. The sorrow and pain he must have felt as the cock crowed was surely heart breaking—the piercing look as he stared into the eyes of his Savior.

What about Paul? The remorse and agony he felt when he realized he had persecuted Christians and his Lord. He had a lifetime to regret this action, but he put it behind him and went on to become a great writer and an apostle.

God wants us to be happy while we are on earth, and He has provided everything to make life joyous. The list is endless—the blessings are boundless.

Lest we become too comfortable, we must remember that this world is not our permanent residence. Isn't this a wonderful thought when we are beset by pain, sorrow, trials, illnesses, disappointments and heartaches?

With God as our Master, guide and leader we will not fear the future. We will keep life in its proper perspective so that we like Paul can say:

I have fought the good fight, I have finished the race, I have kept the faith. Now there is in store for me the crown of righteousness, which the Lord, the righteous Judge, will award to me on that day—and not only to me, but also to all who have longed for his appearing.
—2 Timothy 4:7, 8

Do not let your hearts be troubled. Trust in God; trust also in me. In my Father's house are many rooms; if it were not so, I would have told you. I am going there to prepare a place for you. And if I go and prepare a place for you, I will come back and take you to be with me that you also may be where I am.
—John 14:1-3

25

BLESSINGS OF WINTER

Suddenly the leaves have forsaken the trees and a crisp carpet of brown lays on the ground. The trees, completely bare, are a silhouette of intricate designs against the ice blue sky causing a chill to run through the veins.

In recess until spring the trees still hold a fascination in the various patterns suspended in mid-air which were hidden during the summer by the profuse covering of leaves.

How can anyone doubt there is a Creator?

When I consider your heavens, the work of your fingers, the moon and the stars, which you have set in place.
—Psalm 8:3

The heavens declare the glory of God; the skies proclaim the work of his hands. Day after day they pour forth speech; night after night they display knowledge. There is no speech or language where their voice is not heard. Their voice goes out into all the earth, their words to the ends of the world.
In the heavens he has pitched a tent for the sun, which is like a bridegroom coming forth from his pavilion, like a champion rejoicing to run his course. It rises at one end of the heavens and makes its circuit to the other; nothing is hidden from its heat.
—Psalm 19:1-6

One tree in particular, seen from my den window, has captivated me. I sit in awe at the many pictures I can make in my mind's eye—the small branches entwined in the larger ones, all going in different directions, at the same time keeping a continuity of harmony.

Many people complain when winter comes. It is true that certain hardships are connected with cold weather. Our bodies hurt, our bones are racked with pain if we are old and suffer from arthritis. For the poor and homeless winter is a calamity.

For some winter is a sad and depressing time, but we should remember God has made each season for a purpose and look for the blessings of winter. Winter can be a time of reflection, retreat, renewal and a respite from the activities of a busy spring and summer; perhaps a time to take personal inventory. Changes in habits may need to be made, new goals may need to be set, a change in direction may even need to occur.

The winter months provide more time indoors when we can enjoy great music and good books, especially the Book of books, the Holy Bible. On a dark, gray, rainy day fill your mind and your soul with the wonderful words of life not found anywhere else.

Don't fail to seize the opportunity to observe the nature scene—the bald trees as they display their skeletal structure in contrast to the thick foliage they wear as a façade for summer.

When wintry winds blow and give us an icy kiss when we marvel at the snow as it changes the landscape, and when clouds plant a duskiness in the sky, then it is time to count our blessings and thank God for the quiet moments when our spirits are revived as we study the artistry of the trees and the change in seasons.

After the flood, God made promises to Noah and said:

As long as the earth endures, seedtime and harvest, cold and heat, summer and winter, day and night will never cease.
—Genesis 8:22

It was you [God] who set all the boundaries of the earth; you made both summer and winter.
—Psalm 74:17

Enjoy winter!

GOD'S ESCAPE ROUTE

Escape—fleeing from impending danger—fire, hurricanes, floods, pursuing armies. The word brings fear into our hearts if we are in a path of peril looking for a way out.

The Israelites fled from the army of the Egyptians and God provided the way of escape. David was protected from his enemies because he was a man after God's own heart. God guarded the young man, Joseph, so that he could become the most powerful person in Egypt because he was a righteous man and God had a special purpose for his life.

God delivered Daniel and his companions from the fiery furnace and closed the mouths of the lions to save Daniel. In the New Testament, we read in Acts 5:18, 19 the account of the apostles being thrown in prison and an angel of the Lord opening the doors and bringing them out to safety.

Peter was also delivered by God's angel who shone a light in the prison cell and led him out. Even the iron gate was opened and the angel stayed with Peter until he was near the house of friends.

Does God provide a way of escape for us today? Not in the same way that he made provisions for his people in ancient times. We cannot expect God to shut the mouth of a vicious animal or snatch us from a speeding car if we are in its path.

Our government has laws which if obeyed will help prevent accidents: speed laws, construction site rules, various regulations, all in the interest of public safety. When emergencies arise such as floods, hurricanes, or tornadoes, escape routes are provided and news broadcasts keep us up to date on the situations. Sometimes evacuations are required and it is up to us to heed the warnings and take the necessary precautions for our safety.

In the spiritual realm, God provides escape routes but we have to heed His warnings just as we would in the physical world.

Our God is a God who saves; from the Sovereign Lord comes escape from death.

—Psalm 68:20

We must be aware of the dangers of darkness lurking in the evil mind of Satan. He is busy tempting us in ways of which we are not even aware. The first signal is "watch."

Be always on the watch, and pray that you may be able to escape all that is about to happen, and that you may be able to stand before the Son of Man.
—Luke 21:36

The next admonition is "pray."

Watch and pray so that you will not fall into temptation. The spirit is willing but the body is weak.
—Matthew 26:41

We must be alert at all times, never letting our guard down, and we need to have an active, ongoing prayer life.

Submission to God is required if we want to escape the evils of the world. Only when we make our Holy Father the captain of our ship, the pilot of our plane and our Supreme Leader are we fully equipped to fight the spiritual battle and plan our escape route.

Submit yourselves, then, to God. Resist the devil, and he will flee from you.
—James 4:7

By being a good student of the Bible, studying diligently as for a crucial examination, we will be able to keep from drifting away.

We must pay more careful attention, therefore, to what we have heard, so that we do not drift away.
—Hebrews 2:1

God has put up signposts showing the routes of escape, but we have to look for them and follow the directions. Just as people who refuse to evacuate their homes in times of disaster have to suffer the consequences if they fail to comply, we, too, must be ever vigilant and follow God's escape route.

Flee the evil desires of youth, and pursue righteousness, faith, love and peace, along with those who call on the Lord out of a pure heart.
—2 Timothy 2:22

So, if you think you are standing firm, be careful that you don't fall! No temptation has seized you except what is common to man. And God is faithful; he will not let you be tempted beyond what you can bear. But when you are tempted, he will also provide a way out so that you can stand up under it.
—1 Corinthians 10:12, 13

DON'T RUN AWAY FROM HOME

Since the beginning of life on the earth it seems that someone has been running away from something. After Adam and Eve were tempted to disobey God and ate of the forbidden fruit they tried to hide from God among the trees (Genesis 3:8).

When Sarai, Abram's wife, learned of Hagar's pregnancy she was jealous and mistreated her. In desperation Hagar ran away from home. Near a spring of water the angel of the Lord found Hagar and said,

> And he said, "Hagar, servant of Sarai, where have you come from, and where are you going?"
> "I'm running away from my mistress Sarai," she answered. Then the angel of the Lord told her, "Go back to your mistress and submit to her."
> The angel added, "I will so increase your descendants that they will be too numerous to count."
> —Genesis 16:8-10

After Moses killed the Egyptian who was beating a Hebrew he became afraid and ran away to Midian (Exodus 2:11-15).

In the eighteenth chapter of 1 Kings an intriguing episode took place in the life of Elijah. A confrontation with the prophets of Baal resulted in a demonstration of God's power. The wicked Jezebel threatened to kill Elijah. In fear Elijah ran away and hid completely forgetting the power of God to save him.

Another runaway was Jonah. He was not happy with the assignment that God gave him to preach repentance to the Ninevites.

> But Jonah ran away from the Lord and headed for Tarshish. He went down to Joppa, where he found a ship bound for that port. After paying the fare, he went aboard and sailed for Tarshish to flee from the Lord.
> —Jonah 1:3

The story of the lost son (prodigal) is an example of bad judgment in deciding to leave home. This young man was unwise and headstrong, and only after losing his money and integrity did he realize his mistake.

What are the circumstances that cause people to run away? Fear, rebellion, guilt, sin, misunderstanding—maybe you can name other causes.

The most difficult event to understand regarding desertion is recorded in Matthew, Mark and John. Jesus has been betrayed by one of His own; soldiers andtheir commander along with Jewish officials arrested Jesus.

Then all the disciples deserted him and fled.
—Matthew 26:56b

They ran away! How could they? They had been with Jesus for more than three years. They sat at His feet as He taught the multitudes. They had heard the Sermon on the Mount and the parables; they had witnessed the miracles—even the raising of the dead. They sat with Him at the table for the Last Supper as Jesus instituted the Holy Communion.

Almost unbelievable, isn't it? However, before we become too critical, think—what would you have done if you had been at Gethsemane as the band of soldiers arrived with their swords and staves? We don't really know, but I'm sure that each one of us would like to think that he/she would have been strong enough, loyal enough and determined enough to remain at Christ's side.

Today we still have runaways. Some people run to escape responsibility, some to avoid punishment for crimes committed; others flee from home and family because of misunderstandings and betrayal.

One of the great tragedies involves young people who run away from home. Often the young girls become trapped into prostitution and boys become snared by gangs and drugs.

Some people still try to run away from God, even though they may not realize it.

Still another group who were once faithful Christians have fallen by the wayside. Many things may invade people's lives that cause them to run away from home and the family of God. The world is so much with us and in us that we become trapped and ensnared by Satan.

*So, if you think you are standing firm, be careful that you don't fall!
No temptation has seized you except what is common to man. And
God is faithful; he will not let you be tempted beyond what you can*

bear. But when you are tempted, he will also provide a way out so that you can stand up under it.

—1 Corinthians 10:12, 13

Watch and pray so that you will not fall into temptation. The spirit is willing, but the body is weak.

—Matthew 26:41

Be self-controlled and alert. Your enemy the devil prowls around like a roaring lion looking for someone to devour.

—1 Peter 5:8

Don't run away from home!

THE DEATH OF TIME

*It is I who made the earth and created mankind upon it. My own
hands stretched out the heavens; I marshaled their starry hosts.*
                                                    —Isaiah 45:12

*There is a time for everything, and a season for every activity under
heaven:*
a time to be born and a time to die,
a time to plant and a time to uproot,
a time to kill and a time to heal,
a time to tear down and a time to build,
a time to weep and a time to laugh,
a time to mourn and a time to dance,
*a time to scatter stones and a time to gather
    them,*
a time to embrace and a time to refrain,
a time to search and a time to give up,
a time to keep and a time to throw away,
a time to tear and a time to mend,
a time to be silent and a time to speak,
a time to love and a time to hate,
a time for war and a time for peace.
                                        —Ecclesiastes 3:1-8

When did time begin? Why did it begin? Why did God create
the heavens and the earth? Why did He create man? At what point
did He decide to make the world and everything in it? God has no
timetable and no clock—He is not bound by time.

*With the Lord a day is like a thousand years, and a thousand years
are like a day.*
                                        —2 Peter 3:8

There is no way the human mind can fathom an existence without time, yet with God there is no beginning and no ending—no
time.

The first chapter of Genesis describes the creation and records
the first employment of time. God used six days to bring everything
into being and then rested on the seventh day.

Since we are earthly beings everything revolves around time.
Time to go to bed, time to get up, time to go to work or school, time

for the appointment, time for the game. Often it becomes so hectic that we would like to throw away the clock.

There are times of dread—a time to say goodbye to a son or daughter going away to school or moving to another place. A time to wave to the soldier going to a faraway land. A time when tears fall over a broken heart; a time of grief as we watch the life of a loved one slowly slip away.

Jesus, too, had to face times of dread.

> *Go into the city to a certain man and tell him, "The Teacher says: My appointed time is near. I am going to celebrate the Passover with my disciples at your house."*
> —Matthew 26:18

As the time of His crucifixion drew near I imagine that Jesus dreaded the time He must face—the betrayal, the mockery, the pain, the suffering, the rejection, forsaken by all.

In the garden the disciples fell asleep, perhaps oblivious to what was about to take place.

> *Then he returned to the disciples and said to them, "Are you still sleeping and resting? Look, the hour is near, and the Son of Man is betrayed into the hands of sinners."*
> —Matthew 26:45

In addition to the agony of the cross He also had to endure the time as His mother, Mary, prostrate in grief, wept at the foot of the cross.

> *When He had led them out to the vicinity of Bethany, he lifted up his hands and blessed them. While he was blessing them, he left them and was taken up into heaven.*
> —Luke 24:50, 51

> *After he said this, he was taken up before their very eyes, and a cloud hid him from their sight.*
> —Acts 1:9

In addition to keeping time schedules what other effects does time have on us? It finally robs us of youth, diminishes our eyesight and hearing, deprives us of physical strength. These things should remind us of life's brevity and cause us to welcome the demise of time.

What is your life? You are a mist that appears for a little while and then vanishes.

—James 4:14

At the very moment of our death, time as we know it stops for us. This should not be feared or dreaded. Rather if we have been faithful, we can rejoice in the death of time as we are carried on angels' wings into the realms of timeless day where we will sit at the feet of our Lord and sing praises forever and forever—no end.

Paul's discourse to Timothy:

For I am already being poured out like a drink offering, and the time has come for my departure. I have fought the good fight, I have finished the race, I have kept the faith. Now there is in store for me the crown of righteousness, which the Lord, the righteous Judge, will award to me on that day—and not only to me, but also to all who have longed for his appearing.

—2 Timothy 4:6-8

THE HIDDEN TREASURE

Children of all ages like stories about buried treasures. They never tire of reading them and in an imaginary journey they follow the directions on the maps supposedly leading to the buried treasure.

In the days of the Old West many men sometimes spent their lives looking in caves and mountains for buried treasures. They would buy maps which were supposed to reveal the location of gold and other valuables. The maps were usually fakes and left many men disappointed and disillusioned.

Sunken ships and boats still hold many people captive in the search for treasures buried beneath the seas and oceans. Companies have been formed and large sums of money spent on equipment to probe the depths in an effort to find lost treasures.

Are we looking for a hidden treasure or are we leaving this to someone else?

> *Ask and it will be given to you; seek and you will find; knock and the door will be opened to you. For everyone who asks receives; he who seeks finds; and to him who knocks, the door will be opened.*
> —Matthew 7:7, 8

In the fifth and sixth chapters of Matthew, Jesus sat down on a mountainside and began teaching His disciples and crowds of people. One of His statements was: "For where your treasure is, there your heart will be also." This teaching was in regard to storing up treasures in heaven instead of here on earth.

But the Bible speaks of a hidden treasure. What is it? Where can we find it?

> *My son, if you accept my words and store up my commands within you, turning your ear to wisdom and applying your heart to understanding, and if you call out for insight and cry aloud for understanding, and if you look for it as for silver and search for it as for hidden treasure, then you will understand the fear of the Lord and find the knowledge of God. For the Lord gives wisdom, and from his mouth come knowledge and understanding.*
> —Proverbs 2:1-6

> *Get wisdom, get understanding; do not forget my words or swerve from them. Do not forsake wisdom, and she will protect you; love*

her, and she will watch over you. Wisdom is supreme; therefore get wisdom.
—Proverbs 4:5-7

The wise in heart are called discerning, and pleasant words promote instruction.
—Proverbs 16:21

Let the wise listen and add to their learning.
—Proverbs 1:5

One of the most amazing events of Solomon's life took place at Gibeon.

At Gibeon the Lord appeared to Solomon during the night in a dream, and God said, "Ask for whatever you want me to give you." Solomon answered, "You have shown great kindness to your servant, my father David, because he was faithful to you and righteous and upright in heart. You have continued this great kindness to him and have given him a son to sit on his throne this very day. Now, O Lord my God, you have made your servant king in place of my father David. But I am only a little child and do not know how to carry out my duties. So give your servant a discerning heart to govern your people and to distinguish between right and wrong. For who is able to govern this great people of yours?"
The Lord was pleased that Solomon had asked for this. So God said to him, "Since you have asked for this and not for long life or wealth for yourself, nor have asked for the death of your enemies but for discernment in administering justice, I will do what you have asked. I will give you a wise and discerning heart, so that there will never have been anyone like you, nor will there ever be. Moreover, I will give you what you have not asked for—both riches and honor—so that in your lifetime you will have no equal among kings."
—1 Kings 3:5, 6, 7, 9-13

God speaking to Daniel in a vision:

Those who are wise [or who impart wisdom] will shine like the brightness of the heavens, and those who lead many to righteousness, like the stars for ever and ever.
—Daniel 12:3

Paul speaking to Timothy, his protégé and son in the Lord:

37

And how from infancy you have known the holy Scriptures, which
are able to make you wise for salvation through faith in Christ Jesus.
                                                            —2 Timothy 3:15

During the time of Paul's house arrest he wrote the letter to the
Colossians who were steeped in paganism. Paul urged them to set
their hearts and minds on Christ Jesus:

For this reason, since the day we heard about you, we have not
stopped praying for you and asking God to fill you with the knowl-
edge of his will through all spiritual wisdom and understanding.
                                                            —Colossians 1:9

Since God's word puts so much emphasis on wisdom then we
must look for this hidden treasure. Why? Because wisdom will lead
us to a knowledge of God and His plans for us. Through study and
prayer we will gain this wisdom that puts us in touch with Christ Jesus and His saving power and grace. And wisdom, the hidden
treasure shows us the way to live the Christian life.

Make haste! We have a hidden treasure to find.

SADNESS vs. GLADNESS

"Every cloud has a silver lining" is an old saying. Another is, "Into every life some rain must fall."

There are numerous accounts in the Bible of sadness later becoming gladness. Have you ever thought how Abraham must have felt when God asked him to offer his son, Isaac, as a sacrifice? The sadness that engulfed him must have been almost unbearable. Isaac was the beloved son, the son of Abraham's old age. Now is he to be deprived of him? Then at the lowest point of that dark moment of sadness the angel of the Lord said,

> *"Do not lay a hand on the boy," he said. Do not do anything to him. Now I know that you fear God, because you have not withheld from me your son, your only son.*
> —Genesis 22:12

I imagine that gratitude and gladness swept over Abraham immediately—complete relief.

The exciting story of Joseph's life has fascinated me since childhood. The sadness he must have felt to be sold by his brothers and taken captive to Egypt—, then later unjustly imprisoned. The fear and loneliness he endured for a long time before he was finally given a place of power and distinction.

Joseph must have spent many years wondering about the welfare of his father—he must have been overwhelmed at times with sadness. But this story had a happy ending when the brothers came to Egypt to buy grain and Joseph learned that his father was alive. He also made peace with his brothers who had badly mistreated him.

There is no story in the Bible about any one person that is filled with so much pathos as that of Job. Everything was taken from him—everything except his life. In addition, he was afflicted with boils over his entire body and his wife in desperation said to him:

> *Are you still holding on to your integrity? Curse God and die!*
> —Job 2:9

Job's three friends censured him severely and gave him no comfort. They said that his troubles were caused by his sin.

39

In due time Job's prosperity was restored—twice as much as before. He was blessed with seven sons and three daughters and his life was even better than before—sadness turned to gladness.

The disciples of Jesus were overcome with sadness when they learned that He was to be crucified. Even though they had been with Jesus during His public ministry and had witnessed the miracles they still were confused and bewildered. They did not understand when He said that He would be raised from the dead and go back to the Father. In desperation they asked, "Where will we go? To whom shall we go? To whom shall we turn?"

This was indeed a sad hour, but gradually the sadness was turned to gladness when Christ explained that He would send the Comforter.

But the Counselor, the Holy Spirit, whom the Father will send in my name, will teach you all things and will remind you of everything I have said to you. Peace I leave with you; my peace I give you. I do not give to you as the world gives. Do not let your hearts be troubled and do not be afraid.

—John 14:26, 27

When he had led them out to the vicinity of Bethany, he lifted up his hands and blessed them. While he was blessing them, he left them and was taken up into heaven. Then they worshiped him and returned to Jerusalem with great joy. And they stayed continually at the temple, praising God.

—Luke 24:50-53

The great apostle, Paul, had mountains of sadness in his life. Imagine his agony when he realized he had persecuted the Savior.

I have worked much harder, been in prison more frequently, been flogged more severely, and been exposed to death again and again. Five times I received from the Jews the forty lashes minus one. Three times I was beaten with rods, once I was stoned, three times I was shipwrecked, I spent a night and a day in the open sea.

—2 Corinthians 11:23-25

Paul goes on to say that he has been in constant danger from rivers, bandits, his own countrymen, the Gentiles and from false brothers. He had also suffered from hunger and thirst, and from cold.

What brings sadness into our lives? Many, many things—failure, disappointment, betrayal, illness, consequences of sin, either our own or those of loved ones. Death probably inflicts the greatest sorrow.

Death is our enemy—a separation that transforms the physical to the spiritual. We don't understand it! We can't understand it!

The last enemy to be destroyed is death.
—1 Corinthians 15:26

I declare to you, brothers, that flesh and blood cannot inherit the kingdom of God, nor does the perishable inherit the imperishable. For the perishable must clothe itself with the imperishable, and the mortal with immortality. When the perishable has been clothed with the imperishable, and the mortal with immortality, then the saying that is written will come true: "Death has been swallowed up in victory. Where, O death, is your victory? Where, O death, is your sting?"
—1 Corinthians 15:50, 53-55

Paul was ready to die but at the same time felt the need to remain in the flesh to fulfill his mission.

For to me, to live is Christ and to die is gain. I am torn between the two: I desire to depart and be with Christ, which is better by far; but it is more necessary for you that I remain in the body.
—Philippians 1:21, 23, 24

When the sadness of life comes as it inevitably will, we allow faith to take over so that sorrow will be converted to happiness. Then we can say with Paul:

I have fought the good fight, I have finished the race, I have kept the faith. Now there is in store for me the crown of righteousness, which the Lord, the righteous Judge, will award to me on that day—and not only to me, but also to all who have longed for his appearing.
—2 Timothy 4:7, 8

THE CAVE OF GLORIFICATION

Caves hold a certain fascination for many people which is evidenced by the number of tourists visiting them each year. Carlsbad Caverns in the West, Mammoth Cave in Kentucky and Luray Caverns in Virginia are among some of the most famous.

Spelunkers are so intrigued by caves that they often take great risks to explore them. For me, even though they are beautiful, caves have an ominous and foreboding feeling. The stalactites which hang from the roof of the caves look like daggers ready to pierce the top of my head while the stalagmites rising from the floor appear as nails poised for attack.

Nevertheless, caves have played an important part in life down through the ages. Caves were abundant in the ancient Middle East and served as homes, places of refuge, tombs and even prisons and places of worship.

In Genesis 19:30 we are told that Lot lived in a cave temporarily after escaping the destruction of Sodom. After the death of Sarah, Abraham sought a burial place and approached the Hittites:

> Then Abraham rose from beside his dead wife and spoke to the Hittites. He said, "I am an alien and a stranger among you. Sell me some property for a burial site here so I can bury my dead."
> —Genesis 23:3, 4

The Hittites were very kind and offered their choicest tomb. Abraham asked to buy the cave of Machpelah. Ephron wanted to give him the field and the cave but Abraham insisted on paying 400 shekels of silver.

> So Ephron's field in Machpelah near Mamre—both the field and the cave in it, and all the trees within the borders of the field—was deeded to Abraham as his property in the presence of all the Hittites who had come to the gate of the city.
> —Genesis 23:17, 18

In 1 Samuel 21 and 22 we read the account of David as he fled in fear from Saul and the king of Gath. He escaped to the cave of Adullam. A very interesting story is found in 1 Samuel 24 regarding Saul and David. Saul entered a cave not knowing that David and his men were far back in the cave. David crept up unnoticed and cut off a corner of Saul's robe, but did not take his life.

Another incident of a cave being a source of refuge is found in 1 Kings 19. Fearing Jezebel, Elijah ran for his life and was ready to give up and die when an angel appeared to feed him and sustain him. He then traveled forty days and forty nights until he reached Mt. Horeb and spent the night there in a cave.

The New Testament is filled with accounts of the prominence of caves. In Nazareth many houses were built over caves which provided natural basements. In times of persecution Christians worshiped in caves, and from hieroglyphics we know that codes and messages were carved on the walls of caves.

When Jesus was a young boy He probably knew the locations of many caves, and after His ministry began He may have sought refuge and rest in one of these caves.

The tomb of Lazarus was a cave.

*Jesus, once more deeply moved, came to the tomb. It
was a cave with a stone laid across the entrance.*
—John 11:38

Have you ever stopped to realize that the most important event in human history took place in a manmade cave hewn from a huge rock?

Joseph of Arimathea had prepared a tomb for himself and it had never been used, making it an appropriate place for the burial place of our Lord, Jesus the Christ—the Savior. The poignant account of Christ's burial is told in Matthew, Mark, Luke and John.

Matthew tells us that Joseph of Arimathea was a rich man and a disciple. He asked Pilate for the body of Jesus and wrapped it in a clean linen cloth. John says that Joseph was accompanied by Nicodemus, the man who earlier had visited Jesus at night, and he had brought myrrh and aloes for anointment. Both of them wrapped His body in strips of linen.

The love and compassion of Mary Magdalene, Mary the mother of James, and Salome is shown as they came to the tomb on the first day of the week with spices to anoint Jesus' body.

*When the Sabbath was over, Mary Magdalene, Mary the mother of
James, and Salome bought spices so that they might go to anoint Jesus' body. Very early on the first day of the week, just after sunrise,
they were on their way to the tomb and they asked each other, "Who*

43

will roll the stone away from the entrance of the tomb?" But when they looked up, they saw that the stone, which was very large, had been rolled away. As they entered the tomb, they saw a young man dressed in a white robe sitting on the right side, and they were alarmed. "Don't be alarmed," he said. "You are looking for Jesus the Nazarene, who was crucified. He has risen! He is not here. See the place where they laid him. But go, tell his disciples and Peter, "He is going ahead of you into Galilee. There you will see him, just as he told you."

—Mark 16:1-7

All four writers tell of the angel appearing at the tomb and announcing that Christ had risen. Imagine the anxiety and confusion that they felt as they left the empty tomb.

Luke's account:

Suddenly two men in clothes that gleamed like lightning stood beside them. In their fright the women bowed down with their faces to the ground, but the men said to them, "Why do you look for the living among the dead? He is not here; he has risen! Remember how he told you, while he was still with you in Galilee: 'The Son of Man must be delivered into the hands of sinful men, be crucified and on the third day be raised again.'" Then they remembered his words.

—Luke 24:4-8

The women then went and told the apostles but they did not believe; however, Peter immediately got up and ran to the tomb, saw the strips of linen lying separately and wondered what had happened.

Do we sometimes feel annoyed that the disciples had such difficulty believing Jesus? He had told them repeatedly that His kingdom was not of this world and that He had to suffer the agony, shame and pain of the cross. He told them that He would rise on the third day but they did not comprehend.

Do we think if we had been a disciple and had listened daily to His teaching that we would never had doubt? I wonder.

John 20:1-9 records the incident when Peter raced with John to the tomb and although John arrived first and looked in the tomb he did not go in. Peter did not hesitate to go in and he found the burial cloths. Verse 9 says that they still did not understand from Scripture that Jesus had to rise from the dead.

What is the first thing you want to know when you reach your heavenly home? There are many things that I want to ask about but

44

after much thought I want my Savior to give a detailed description of His resurrection.

The resurrection was the culmination of Christ's earthly ministry—the decisive point and the summit of His purpose for taking the human form and making the supreme sacrifice for sinful mankind. We emphasize the cross, the agony, the ridicule and scorn, forsaken by all as He bore the sins of the whole world, but this would be nothing without the resurrection.

As the splendor and radiance spread through the dark cave, as He removed the linen cloth from His head and as He unwound the strips from around His body, our guarantee of salvation and eternal life—it was too holy for human eyes to behold but the evidence was all-conclusive as Jesus appeared to His disciples and the women.

At last they understood what Christ had been teaching them—that His Kingdom was not a worldly one—that only by His crucifixion, resurrection and ascension could there be salvation and a heavenly abode.

We must not fear death for we know that just as the cave was filled with indescribable radiance and glory we, too, will experience the magnificent resurrection to eternal life.

BROKEN LIVES RESTORED

During the last several decades there has been a revival in the restoration of old houses and buildings. People have realized the value of bringing back dilapidated houses to their former charm and usefulness. Old historical buildings have been restored to their former grandeur and have been placed on the Register for Preservation of Historical Places.

I like antiques—some better than others. I'm now enjoying several beautiful old pieces of furniture which belonged in my mother's family, the result of restoration by my son-in-law. He is very good at repairing and restoring otherwise discarded pieces of furniture to their former appearance.

Old crumbly houses, standing silent for years, come to life again when restored. Sounds of laughter and activities once again vibrate through the walls—a house saved from the dump heap.

After restoration, perhaps taking several years, neglected, deserted buildings ravaged by wind and rain coming through broken windows will reverberate with movement; a former school may become a business office; a church building may become a home; a factory may become a museum.

What about broken lives? Can they be restored and repaired? Many things can cause fractures that eventually break our lives asunder—death of loved ones, illness of family members or yourself, separation, failure, sin, financial losses, divorce, abuse—things that bring changes of traumatic proportion.

People react in different ways when lives are torn apart. Some withdraw into themselves, not wanting to share their misfortune with others. Another group tries to pretend that nothing is wrong, perhaps because of embarrassment. A few will say, "I don't want to burden my friends with my troubles." Suicide is more prevalent than ever before, or so it seems. In desperation some people take their own lives rather than face financial loss or the shame that may come from embarrassing events. In extreme cases, there are those who choose to leave the country, even changing their identity.

Why are people so hesitant to take their problems to God? He, and He alone, has the healing power, the compassion, the love and mercy to bring order to confused lives.

All of us can quote the 23rd Psalm from memory, but do we really believe it when we find our lives in shambles? "He leads me beside quiet waters, He restores my soul." Another scripture, less familiar perhaps, reads, "Restore to me the joy of your salvation and grant me a willing spirit, to sustain me" (Psalm 51:12).

Restoration, whether it be buildings or lives, is a difficult process. Decayed walls must be torn down, bricks replaced, fresh paint applied, new fixtures attached. Restored lives require changes—changes in attitude and perspective, as in the case of a terminal illness. When sin has taken over, habits and companions must change. Alteration of lifestyle may be required when a business fails, and a change of location may be necessary after a divorce or a death.

Remember the song, "Bring Christ Your Broken Life"? It is a very comforting song. Christ wants you to bring to Him your broken life, empty wasted years, every care, haunting fear and nameless dread.

All of us will have fractures in our lives, some worse than others. There will be broken dreams, broken hearts, broken homes, broken promises. Bare your soul and ask Him to help you mend your broken life. Whatever you can do to heal the breaks resolve to do your part, then leave the rest in God's hands.

Nothing is more consoling than the proper song at the right time. We often fail to realize the importance of singing. Why did the Lord command us to sing? To comfort us and those around us as well as to praise Him for His boundless mercy and blessings. One example is, "When Storms Around Are Sweeping."

Are you taking advantage of your right to pray? You have constant access to God's throne room. He made this possible when you accepted Christ as your Savior, obeyed in baptism and received His Spirit.

You may become devastated by a broken life but you can be completely restored. God will help you put the fractured pieces together again. You will be "good as new," and even the cracks won't show. Your life can take on new meaning and your spiritual life will be stronger than ever. You will experience a closer relationship with God.

Why am I so confident of these things? I, too, have been surrounded by the surging seas of painful, debilitating illnesses and life-threatening operations. God rescued me from the raging waters of death and despair, restored my soul and sheltered me in His arms. He will do the same for you.

THE TREASURE STOREHOUSE

What comes to mind when you hear the word "treasure"? Many of us would think of great riches, silver and gold, things to be desired and hoarded. We might think also of buried treasures, perhaps beneath the sea. There are people who spend much time and money seeking treasures lost at sea due to shipwreck.

What do you treasure and where are your treasures? The Holy Word tells us what not to do and what to do regarding treasures.

> Do not store up for yourselves treasures on earth, where moth and rust destroy, and where thieves break in and steal. But store up for yourselves treasures in heaven, where moth and rust do not destroy, and where thieves do not break in and steal. For where your treasure is, there your heart will be also.
> —Matthew 6:19-21

Are we following these instructions, or are we caught up in the accumulation of material possessions? We are so human that sometimes we forget this earth is not our home; we are only traveling through.

How do we store up treasures in heaven? Does the concept seem unrealistic and difficult? If we set our goal on things above it will not be as hard as we might think.

Our acts of faith and obedience as God's children are treasures that God places at His throne. As we read and study the Bible daily, we mature in our knowledge and understanding of the Holy Scriptures producing a fragrant aroma that ascends and finds its place in our storehouse of treasures. Our prayers also go up to heaven in the form of sweet incense.

> May my prayer be set before you like incense; may the lifting up of my hands be like the evening sacrifice.
> —Psalm 141:2

Another treasure goes into our storehouse when we become selfless as opposed to being self-centered. This is accomplished as we become aware of the needs of others and do everything we can to help, encourage and serve our fellow man.

By spreading the gospel and sharing our faith and convictions with others we are adding other treasures to our storehouses. This does not mean we are working our way to heaven as we are unable to do that; only through God's grace and mercy can we be saved, only the sacrifice of Christ for our sins is our atonement.

After we add the fruit of the Spirit—love, joy, peace, patience, kindness, goodness, faithfulness, gentleness and self-control, we will have a formula that fills our treasure chest while we are pilgrims on this earth as well as for eternal life.

> *The Lord is exalted, for he dwells on high; he will fill Zion with justice and righteousness. He will be the sure foundation for your times, a rich store of salvation and wisdom and knowledge; the fear of the Lord is the key to this treasure.*
> —Isaiah 33:5, 6

IN A HOLDING PATTERN

Definition: standing still, not moving, caught in a time frame. What does it mean regarding the Christian life? Is it possible that we are standing still and satisfied with the status quo? Maybe we don't realize that we have become complacent and are in a holding pattern.

Let's take inventory and explore our spiritual well being. Perhaps it's time to have a more open mind; time to cast aside prejudices, unauthorized traditions and preconceived ideas—not making unjust and unfounded criticism of fellow Christians.

Instead of relying on who said what and when, we must go to the Holy Word. The way of salvation and the manner of life we are to follow as Christians is laid out in plain terms and everyday language.

> *Continue to work out your salvation with fear and trembling, for it is God who works in you to will and to act according to his good purpose.*
> —Philippians 2:12, 13

The Bible tells us that we must worship in spirit and in truth. We need to make sure that we do not add anything not authorized or subtract anything that is authorized. Some things are left to good judgment and are matters of opinion.

I hesitate to say the word "change." For some it is disturbing and unsettling. Is it possible that we have become too set in our ways?

Do I hear someone saying, "What's wrong with singing two songs, having a prayer, another song and the sermon? I've always done it that way." There's nothing wrong with this order of worship, but it isn't the only way. What is expedient for one congregation might not be for another. We don't have a right to criticize unless a commandment has been violated. Communion can be before the sermon or after. Our monetary gifts can be taken at any time, keeping in mind that everything is done in decency and in order.

Let's think about our hymns. Many people don't like the new songs; they have closed their minds. Do you know that at one time "Amazing Grace" was a new song and was considered too contemporary? It was a long time before it "caught on" but now it is considered one of the most loved songs of all time.

Even though I am well past three score and ten years, I like many of the new songs. This may be due in part to the fact that I have written some hymns. What we must consider is the substance contained in the hymns whether or not the words are meaningful and relevant, not if they were written a hundred years ago or yesterday.

Please don't have a closed mind about new songs. Some are very spiritually uplifting and more significant. Let's balance our worship with some old and some new. We don't want to remain in a holding pattern.

Our hymns can be projected on a screen. This is very good for those who have poor vision. They can be printed in program form with page numbers given or they can be announced by the song leader.

We cannot avoid change—everything changes; that is, except God and His Word. His laws never change, the way to salvation does not change.

> There is one body and one Spirit—just as you were called to one
> hope when you were called—one Lord, one faith, one baptism; one
> God and Father of all, who is over all and through all and in all.
> —Ephesians 4:4, 5

Our physical bodies change, technology changes, culture and customs change. There was a time when church buildings had two front entrances, one for men and one for women. Men and women did not sit together—families were separated by gender.

Later many people were of the opinion that it was wrong to have a kitchen in the church building until it was realized the building is not sacred. One change I'm very glad that has taken place is eliminating the single cup for the fruit of the vine. Don't you agree?

One of our greatest blessings is living under the New Covenant, the law of freedom in Christ. We don't have to offer animal sacrifices, observe special feast days or have our sins rolled forward, and we aren't burdened with numerous requirements under the old law.

With this in mind we must not become encumbered with unauthorized traditions and practices.

Don't be caught in a holding pattern—live with the open Bible!

51

THE DIVINE FEAST

What goes through your mind when you hear the word "feast"? Most people would describe an elaborate banquet table set with fine china and sterling silver; the food would be rich, abundant, and attractively displayed on large silver trays.

There is another feast that is very different. It is the spiritual feast, the Lord's Supper—Holy Communion, consisting only of unleavened bread and fruit of the vine. The time that we come closest to our Savior, Jesus the Christ, is on the first day of the week as we gather to partake of this divine feast.

This act of worship may be the hardest to achieve, as it is very difficult to prepare ourselves for this occasion and to focus on the true meaning of the Lord's Supper. It is the time to concentrate on Christ's suffering and His supreme sacrifice for sinful mankind; therefore, our attitude must be one of gratitude.

We come to the feast in humility aware of our vulnerability and our dependence, and with contrite hearts. God calls us to righteousness, and it is a time of renewal to Christ and an affirmation to our fellow Christians that we are consecrated to a life of service in His kingdom.

It is the time to reflect on the glorious resurrection that gives us the promise of eternal life and the hope of sitting at the heavenly table with Him and the redeemed of all ages, looking forward with eager anticipation to Christ's coming again to claim us as His own.

Communion is a time to look inward, examine our lives, confess our sins, and renew our commitment. An outward action also takes place as we share this holy act of worship with fellow Christians. Each person strengthens another and a bond is formed that unites us as the family of God. Sitting quietly and reverently during the communion emphasizes the seriousness and solemnity of the occasion and is a good example to those around us, especially children and young people.

May we determine this very day that we will begin preparing our hearts and minds before we arrive at the meeting place on the Lord's Day so that we will worship in spirit and in truth; so that we will participate in the feast divine in a manner pleasing to our heavenly Father.

PATCHWORK OF LIFE

I think that most people admire a handmade quilt whether or not they are quilters. Incidentally, we usually think of quilting as an art form for women, but the most beautiful quilts I have ever seen were made by men.

We are amazed as we examine the different shapes and color combinations pieced together and held with tiny stitches. When the early settlers came to the New World they brought quilts with them as they were prized possessions. Many of the designs used today were brought to this country from Europe and the British Isles.

I haven't been a quilter very long but this art form has brought me much pleasure and also warm quilts for my grandsons. A special bond exists with quilters—strangers immediately become friends as they share designs, ideas, and techniques.

Have you ever thought that your life is very much like a quilt? Many characteristics make up your personality and your value system. So, let's pretend and make a spiritual quilt. The design is the first decision to be made. I don't think that we want to make a Crazy Quilt made by many people in the 1700-1800's. It consisted of odd shaped pieces put together in haphazard fashion with no distinct design, no order or continuity and no thought of colors. This quilt was made of scraps and out of necessity; what it lacked in beauty was made up for in warmth.

We want our quilt to exemplify our lives as we follow the plan and purpose that God has for us. With this in mind we must be careful as we choose each block. We will call our quilt a Sampler as each block will be different.

The first block will be joy. Everyone likes a cheerful person, someone pleasant to be around. God expects us to be happy and cheerful so that we can let our light shine.

You have made known to me the path of life; you will fill me with joy in your presence.
                                                               —Psalm 16:11

Next comes kindness which brings to mind the will to do good and to treat others the way we wish to be treated—always with gentleness and consideration.

Be kind and compassionate to one another, forgiving each other, just as in Christ God forgave you.
—Ephesians 4:32

A block of patience should be added now and this one may be hard to fit in. It is so difficult to wait, whether it is waiting in line or anticipating a special event. Even in our prayers we expect answers immediately but God may be saying, "Wait."

Be still before the Lord and wait patiently for him.
—Psalm 37:7

I wait for the Lord, my soul waits, and in his word I put my hope.
—Psalm 130:5

The next block is love, and it should be placed in the center just as love needs to be the core of our lives. Love does not keep records of wrongs inflicted. It always forgives, trusts, hopes and perseveres. Isn't this wonderful?

Christ is the supreme example of love.

For God so loved the world that he gave his one and only Son, that whoever believes in him shall not perish but have eternal life.
—John 3:16

And now these three remain: faith, hope and love. But the greatest of these is love.
—1 Corinthians 13:13

The thirteenth chapter of 1 Corinthians is known as the "love" chapter. In it we read that love is patient, kind, does not envy nor boast, and is not proud, not rude, nor self-seeking, not easily angered.

Peace will be our next block. All of us desire peace—in the family, with friends and neighbors, in the family of God and peace in the world. During the Christmas season we sing, "Peace on earth, good will to men," inspired by our Savior, Jesus, the Prince of Peace.

Turn from evil and do good; seek peace and pursue it.
—Psalm 34:14

Peace I leave with you; my peace I give you. I do not give to you as the world gives. Do not let your hearts be troubled and do not be afraid.
—John 14:27

Therefore, since we have been justified through faith, we have peace
with God through our Lord Jesus Christ.
—Romans 5:1

A block of humility will be an important block in our quilt. Humility is not pretending to be important even if we are. All of us are self-centered at times and we may brag without realizing how this comes across to others. Some people are naturally humble, others have to work at it. The Bible tells us the value of humility.

Young men, in the same way be submissive to those who are older.
All of you, clothe yourselves with humility toward one another, be-
cause, 'God opposes the proud but gives grace to the humble.'
—1 Peter 5:5

In order to have a spiritual quilt we must add ablock of self-control. It is not easy to control one's acts, impulses and emotions, but we must try.

For this reason, make every effort to add to your faith goodmess; and
to goodness, knowledge; and to knowledge, self-control; and to self-
control, perseverance; and to perseverance, godliness. . . .
—II Peter 1:5, 6

He who ignores discipline despises himself, but whoever heeds cor-
rection gains understanding.
—Proverbs 15:32

The last block will be goodness. I believe that all of us want to be good, and in order to have excellent character we must have goodness. In the beautiful 23rd Psalm David writes that since the Lord is his shepherd he feels that goodness and love (mercy) will follow him all the days of his life.

It is time to finish our quilt. It will not be perfect; some of the pieces may be a little crooked and off-center; our stitches may not be even in every block because we, as human beings, can never reach perfection but with Christ as our perfect example we can say along with Paul:

I have fought the good fight, I have finished the race, I have kept the
faith.
—2 Timothy 4:7

DON'T ROCK TOO LONG

Making the Most of the Golden Years

It has been said that old age is not for sissies. Some writers speak of "the golden years," while others refer to the "sunset of life." Some people are anxious for retirement, but others dread the thought.

Why is it that some people will not tell their ages? Is this false pride or a fear of old age? We should be grateful for each day, each month, each year that we are permitted to live and not be ashamed of our age. If we have reached the three score and ten we say, "We're living on borrowed time." All of us regardless of age are living on borrowed time. From the moment of birth we began to die. Our lives are brief at best.

> *What is your life? You are a mist that appears for a little while and then vanishes.*
>
> —James 4:14

The people under the old dispensation lived by faith because they knew they were aliens and strangers on earth. I think that we sometimes forget that we are pilgrims on a journey traveling towards a permanent home.

There are those who are so fearful of death that they refuse to talk about it and refuse to make earthly preparations, but it is more important to make spiritual preparation.

We don't live many years until we realize that this world is not Paradise or Utopia. Sooner or later, maybe both, our lives will be overwhelmed with problems, sickness, sadness, tragedy, loss and even chaos.

This being true, do we live in fear and anxiety waiting for something terrible to happen? No—God has given us life and wants us to be happy here. This world is a proving ground and God has given us a formula for happiness, but we must discover the secret ingredients and put them together. Along with the sweet there is the bitter; with the sunshine there is rain and there are storms.

> *Yet man is born to trouble as surely as sparks fly upward.*
>
> —Job 5:7

Man born of woman is of few days and full of trouble. He springs up like a flower and withers away; like a fleeting shadow, he does not endure.

—Job 14:1, 2

We need to fortify ourselves so that we will have the resilience to sustain us when things go awry, otherwise we will not be ready when bad things happen. How many times have you heard, "I never dreamed this would happen to me," or "Why me?"

Develop a positive attitude. Look outward, not inward. Don't dwell on your problems and infirmities. Everyone has them. Don't linger in the past wondering what might have been.

Reaching a certain age is no excuse to give up and give in to the rocking chair. Depending on your health you may have to cut back on some activities and find substitutes. I have a friend who is living with cancer and has undergone a series of chemotherapy treatments but she has not given up, feeling sorry for herself. Instead she visits nursing homes, takes food to shut-ins and the sick and even takes some of these people to doctors' appointments.

Don't say you don't have any talents. Maybe they are hiding and you need to find them. Talents can be developed even in the golden years. Another friend took up painting after she had retired from teaching and is now known for beautiful artwork.

Remember the parable of the talents recorded in Matthew 25:14-28? You must not hide your talents because you have an obligation to use your talents to the best of your ability.

If your vision is still good and you can use your hands there are many things you can do for others. Send someone a note—not just a printed card, but express your own thoughts to fit the situation. It takes a little more time and effort but it is worth it.

Have you been wondering for years what to do with old greeting cards? They are so pretty it is a shame to throw them away. Cut them up and make tray favors for hospitals and nursing homes. A brief scripture can be written on them making them a nice surprise on a food tray.

Many years ago while hospitalized for serious surgery, I received a tray favor made from an old greeting card and it made my day brighter. I didn't know who made it but I thought, "She/he did what they could."

If you can knit, crochet or embroider teach a young person who is eager to learn. Use this talent to make small gifts such as bookmarks, small dolls or animals—these things make perfect remembrances for the sick and shut-in.

I recommend quilting if you haven't already done so. No, you are never too old. I did not make my first until I was 70. It is a most useful and rewarding endeavor. Quilting is very good for retired men also. Some of the most beautiful quilts on display at quilt shows have been made by men.

You haven't found your forte yet? How about painting? You have always wanted to paint, haven't you? Of course you have, so do it. One of my dear friends started painting in her retirement years and now has prize paintings hanging in an art gallery. How about pottery making? This same friend has studied and learned this art form too. Old age doldrums will never overtake her.

You say you have arthritis in your hands? Your vision is still good, though. Read and study some subject you have always been interested in but never had the time until now. Discover again the library and bookstores. Share the things you learn with others. Read and give book reviews to shut-ins who can no longer see well enough to read. This will open up a whole new world to you and the people you share it with.

Learn to be a storyteller—everyone likes a good story whether it be a true one or an imaginary one. This activity keeps the mind alert and brings so much joy. Little children will sit spellbound at the feet of older people to hear a story.

Perhaps your vision isn't as good as it once was. How can you spend your time in a productive way? Listen to tapes of good music; play sermon tapes which can be very uplifting. Share these with others. Call someone just to say, "I'm thinking of you." Your call may be the encouragement that the person needs.

Don't feel that your life is over because of illness, loss of loved ones, serious problems, etc. Don't give up and don't feel sorry for yourself. Are you saying, "But you haven't been through what I have." No, I haven't, but have you been through what I have?

Shattered dreams cannot be mended, but other dreams can be substituted. Shattered lives may appear hopeless at first but with faith and God's help, plus the love and concern of others, a new beginning can be made.

It is not good to look back in regret and say, "I wish I had not done that or I wish I had done this." Spilled milk cannot be put back.

Do you remember the old song, "Accentuate the Positive, Eliminate the Negative"? It is difficult to be positive all the time but we can strive towards that end. Occasionally I hear someone say, "I've lived too long, I'm tired and can no longer handle the pressures and stress." These remarks disturb me.

We must never forget that God is near and ready to help us if we ask. When we sing, "God Will Take Care of You," do we really believe it?

> *Why are you downcast, O my soul? Why so disturbed within me?*
> *Put your hope in God, for I will yet praise him, my Savior and my*
> *God.*
> —Psalm 42:5, 6

Everyone, regardless of age, has to make their own happiness which is only found in service to God and to others. Seek and you will find various ways to serve. Give a smile to someone every day. I think you'll get one back.

All of us need rest and relaxation, and a rocking chair is a good place to revive our spirits and renew our energy, but don't rock too long!

> *Therefore we do not lose heart. Though outwardly we are wasting*
> *away, yet inwardly we are being renewed day by day. For our light*
> *and momentary troubles are achieving for us an eternal glory that*
> *far outweighs them all. So we fix our eyes not on what is seen, but*
> *on what is unseen. For what is seen is temporary, but what is un-*
> *seen is eternal.*
> —2 Corinthians 4:16-18

THE MANTLE OF RIGHTEOUSNESS

Have you ever thought that your clothing reveals many things about you? Your clothes reveal your personality indicating whether you are an introvert or an extrovert; a leader or a follower; whether you are making a statement or blending with the masses. There are, of course, exceptions to these observations.

From the time of the fig leaves until the present time apparel has played an interesting part in our lives. Various cultures and backgrounds bring our differences to light. Clothing has always been distinct relative to race, environment and occupation.

In the Holy Land and in the known world at the time of the Old Testament the tunic was the basic garment. Many had bright colored stripes and were made of wool, linen or cotton. Men's tunics were short whereas women's were to the ankle and mostly blue.

The Bible references to "sackcloth and ashes" meant that the person was in mourning or in a state of repentance or sorrow over trials and tribulations. Sackcloth was uncomfortable and scratchy, as it was a tunic made of goat's hair. Job 1:20 tells us that Job rent his mantle when informed of the death of his children.

Everyone who could afford it had a cloak or mantle that was worn over the tunic especially in cold weather. Garments were sometimes used to pay debts or to barter. Clothing was so valuable that the Jewish law permitted persons to retrieve their garments from a burning building on the Sabbath. The mantle was a person's most valuable possession and also served as a sleeping garment.

A unique experience is recorded in 2 Kings regarding a mantle:

As they [Elijah and Elisha] were walking along and talking together, suddenly a chariot of fire and horses of fire appeared and separated the two of them, and Elijah went up to heaven in a whirlwind. Elisha saw this and cried out, "My father! My father! The chariots and horsemen of Israel!" And Elisha saw him no more. Then he took hold of his own clothes and tore them apart. He picked up the cloak that had fallen from Elijah and went back and stood on the bank of the Jordan. Then he took the cloak that had fallen from him and struck the water with it. "Where now is the Lord, the God of Elijah?" he asked. When he struck the water, it divided to the right and to the left, and he crossed over.

—2 Kings 2:11-14

In the Sermon on the Mount as recorded in Matthew 5:40 and Luke 6:29 Jesus warns against retaliation. He said:

And if someone wants to sue you and take your tunic, let him have your cloak as well.

This would be very hard for a person to do because of the great value of clothing.

In the parable of the wedding feast a guest was thrown out for not wearing wedding clothes, emphasizing the proper use of clothing (Matthew 22).

Christ told His disciples that when they gave clothes to the naked, they were clothing Him (Matthew 25:36). In another vein a prophecy in Psalm 22:18 in regard to Christ's clothing says:

They divide my garments among them and cast lots for my clothing.

We want our spiritual mantle to be the best. What can we surround ourselves in? What garment will completely envelop us and provide protection from the wind of temptation, the rain of despair and the storm of sin?

Lord, who may dwell in your sanctuary? Who may live on your holy hill? He whose walk is blameless and who does what is righteous, who speaks the truth from his heart and has no slander on his tongue.
—Psalm 15:1-3

I was young and now I am old, yet I have never seen the righteous forsaken or their children begging bread.
—Psalm 37:25

The Lord is far from the wicked but he hears the prayer of the righteous.
—Proverbs 15:29

Gray hair is a crown of splendor; it is attained by a righteous life.
—Proverbs 16:31

But unto you that fear my name shall the Sun of righteousness arise with healing in his wings.
—Malachi 4:2 (KJV)

But thanks be to God that, though you used to be slaves to sin, you wholeheartedly obeyed the form of teaching to which you were entrusted. You have been set free from sin and have become slaves to righteousness.

—Romans 6:17, 18

Draw the mantle of righteousness close around you to shield you and protect you.

THE PORCH SWING
(A poignant reminiscence)

During the 20's and 30's, at the time I was growing up in a small town, all houses had porches. At least I can't recall a house without a porch. It was an important part of the house—an extension of the inside.

The back porch, usually screened in, was for utilitarian purposes—storage for various things such as potatoes, apples and nuts, and of course was the place for the icebox. The screen door was kept unlatched on the day the iceman made his delivery so he could put the ice in the box.

The front porch was almost like an enlargement of the parlor. Neighbors and friends came by and visited on the porch. We received the latest news, learned who was sick and who had a new baby. We took handwork to the porch and even green beans to string while we chatted with the people passing by on the sidewalk.

Every porch had a swing, the perfect place for one on one conversations. Everything was discussed from politics and religion to economics and family matters. Two young girls, close friends, would share secrets, giggle about boys and wonder about the "birds and bees."

The porch swing was a place of courtship, holding hands in the moonlight. When the porch light came on you knew it was time to say "goodnight" to your date. Sometimes a quick kiss might be stolen but you knew Mother was peeping out from behind the lace curtains.

Many marriage proposals were made while sitting in the swing and perhaps an engagement ring slipped on the finger of a trembling hand. Unfortunately, unhappy events occurred also—a ring returned or a marriage proposal refused. My own personal experience of having to tell a boyfriend that he was just a friend and that I could not marry him took place in a porch swing.

During my school years we lived in several different houses to be near the school so I could walk. My family did not have a car until I was 18. Remember the depression?

Each house we moved to had a porch, sometimes extending the width of the house and others curving around the side of the house. Each had a swing and still holds many memories for me, but none was quite like a special porch swing.

My uncle lived on a farm in West Tennessee. I spent several weeks each summer during my teen years visiting Uncle Elbert and Aunt Bertie. They had lost their only child at birth and I was special to them as I was the only child remaining in all my mother's family.

The house was typical of that era: white frame, two story with a large porch extending the width of the house. Pots of ferns lined the edge of the porch. A swing was on the left side of the front door and several chairs were placed on the right side. Inside, a hall ran through the center of the house dividing it into two separate sections. The parlor, dining room and kitchen were on the left; three bedrooms on the right. There were two bedrooms upstairs, rarely used.

My room was on the front with one window looking out over the porch. The other window was on the side looking towards a flower and vegetable garden. I loved the gentle breeze coming through the windows and the flutter of the lace curtains dancing in a rhythmic pattern.

Usually I was awakened by the cooing of doves and other birds singing their good-morning greeting along with the clanging of milk buckets as my uncle headed towards the barn to do the morning milking. I knew when he returned we would enjoy a delicious country breakfast and then I could sit in the porch swing. First I asked Aunt Bertie if I could help her and sometimes I went to the garden to gather vegetables, other times she taught me the art of churning butter. Then I was free to slip away to the porch swing.

Uncle Elbert's large cornfield was across the dirt road facing the house which sat a good distance back from the road. I liked to watch the tall green stalks as they grew day by day and the brown silk tassels seemed to wave to me. Occasionally a car passed by, (never more than two or three a day), stirring up dust if the weather was unusually dry. A horn would blow and I waved although I didn't know the occupants of the car.

Sitting in the swing I could shut out the problems of growing up with all the uncertainties and concerns over family situations. There was no schoolwork and no responsibilities for the moment. I could daydream as young girls should in the age of innocence.

I became Cinderella waiting for the Prince to find me so he could place the lost slipper on my foot and sweep me away to live happily everafter. Then I became a princess held captive in a castle by an evil witch, waiting for the knight in shining armor to appear on his white horse to carry me safely away.

After supper (not dinner) I helped with the dishes and then hurried back to the swing to watch the setting sun. Sometimes Uncle Elbert and Aunt Bertie joined me on the porch, but we were silent for the most part as we drank in God's glory watching the sun turn from orange to red before sinking into oblivion until the next day.

It was at this time that I wondered what time and years would bring to my life. Who would I marry? Would there be children? Where would I live? What was ahead of me?

Remember your Creator in the days of your youth, before the days of trouble come and the years approach when you will say "I find no pleasure in them."
—Ecclesiastes 12:1

Sundays were different and special. We got up earlier as we had a long drive to church. Every Sunday morning Aunt Bertie cooked the custard for the ice cream and Uncle Elbert cranked the old fashioned freezer until the cream was frozen. He then wrapped the wooden bucket with a burlap sack and placed it under a shade tree until our return. Sometimes the flavor was fresh peach or strawberry, other times it would be banana or vanilla. It did not matter to me as it was all delicious.

The entire drive to the church building was on a dirt road and sometimes we met a car which sprayed dust everywhere. We were fortunate if we made the trip without meeting a car, which was often the case. If it was raining, my uncle put up the flaps on the sides of the car to keep us dry. The road had many ruts and mud puddles—I think he hit all of them most of the time.

My uncle and aunt were devout Christians. Aunt Bertie taught the young children for Sunday school. Uncle Elbert led most of the prayers. Preaching was once a month as one preacher had to make the circuit of several churches.

After services everyone stayed to visit. There were many things to talk about as usually it would be the following Sunday before the members would see one another again. I often became impatient as my mind began to wander to the ice cream waiting under the shade tree.

Sunday dinner was fried chicken, biscuits, brown gravy, several vegetables and THE ice cream. The porch swing was waiting for me and I took up residence again to resume my dreams and ponderings. The dog, Busy, joined me at times when she wasn't following my uncle. Busy was a small, white, short-haired dog of unknown pedigree and I enjoyed her company.

I did not realize at the time how fortunate I was to have been born into a Christian family. It was not until years later that I realized the full impact that Uncle Elbert and Aunt Bertie had on my life. Whether visiting or at home I never questioned church attendance. It was understood that we went if possible.

At age 12 I was baptized and although I was serious about the matter it was not until I matured spiritually that I became aware of what life is and the purpose for being. Of course, I'm sure this is true of all young people.

The weeks soon passed and it was time to return home and go back to school. The years seemed to go more quickly as I approached the adult years, and for a time the porch swing was forgotten. I married and the war came. My husband Clarence spent three years in the Army Air Force and I traveled with him during this time, living in six different places.

In 1951, after eleven years of marriage, our daughter, Lynn, was born. She blessed our lives in ways too numerous to name. Life took on new meaning and new purposes. My teen years had been filed away and saved to recall another day.

Trips to the farm were few and far between; however, Uncle Elbert and Aunt Bertie did live to see our daughter. When she was two we visited them and for a brief time I held Lynn on my lap as we sat in the porch swing. That was the last time.

The younger generations have missed so much if they don't have a porch swing or a special place during the teen years to muse, dream and contemplate. It might be a tree house or a quiet place near a stream—it just happened to be a swing on the porch of a white farmhouse for me. What was it for you?

Not only in youth but throughout our lives we need a place of refuge from time to time where we can quietly take inventory of our lives and reflect on our spiritual maturity.

LOOKING FOR BUNNIES

The trees of the Lord are well watered, the cedars of Lebanon that he planted. There the birds make their nests; the stork has its home in the pine trees. The high mountains belong to the wild goats; the crags are a refuge for the coneys.

—Psalm 104:16-18

My youngest grandson has been interested in nature almost from day one. Before he could walk he sat on my lap as we looked out from double windows over my backyard which is enclosed by a high hedge. Even though I did not know how much he understood, I told him that God made the grass, trees, flowers, birds and animals.

When Nathan learned to walk he went directly to the window. He was very interested in the birds and became excited as they flew away after pecking in the grass. The squirrels held a special fascination UNTIL he spotted his first bunny. He was not talking at the time but he pointed and jabbered and I knew he wanted to know what it was. I said, "Bunny," and then I told him all I knew about rabbits and bunnies (which isn't much) and I wondered how much he was able to comprehend.

Nathan began talking, finally, and I encouraged him to say, "bird" and "bunny." The word "squirrel" was too difficult for him so we didn't attempt to pronounce it. Soon he was saying "bird" and "bunny" with a special emphasis on "bunny."

Nathan grew and the seasons changed. The trees released their leaves making a brown, crunchy carpet on the ground. The air became crisp leading to cold, windy days. All things in nature began to retreat, sending a message that it was time to rest. One day Nathan said, "Where are the bunnies?" I explained that the rabbits had gone to their burrows for the winter and that we probably would not see them until the next spring. I told him we would have to wait until the grass started turning green and the leaves began to appear on the trees before we would see bunnies again.

For the most part I soon forgot about things outside and I assumed Nathan had too. When he came to my house we played games and read books. Then one early spring day he looked out the window and said, "The grass is getting green." I said, "Yes, and the leaves are beginning to come out on the trees." He turned to me and said, quizzically, "Seen any bunnies?" Even though it had been four or five months he remembered my words. I will never forget that moment.

When Nathan was in kindergarten I often picked him up in the afternoons. Our route was on Granny White Pike and in the spring the white and pink dogwoods are beautiful. I pointed them out and said that they were dogwood trees. His immediate question was, "Why is it called dogwood?" I didn't have the answer and still don't. I suggested that we count the dogwood trees between the school and my house, keeping the number of pinks and whites separate. He liked the idea and we compared the numbers every few days. Nathan still notices the dogwood trees in springtime.

This may seem like a small thing, but I think a love of nature is important. Nature's thread is woven throughout the Bible and intertwines in our lives for a reason.

> *Blessed is the man who does not walk in the counsel of the wicked or stand in the way of sinners or sit in the seat of mockers. He is like a tree planted by streams of water, which yields its fruit in season and whose leaf does not wither. Whatever he does prospers.*
>
> —Psalm 1:1, 3

In the allegorical book, Song of Songs, the beauties and benefits of nature are described in magnificent language.

> *See! The winter is past; the rains are over and gone. Flowers appear on the earth; the season of singing has come, the cooing of doves is heard in our land. The fig tree forms its early fruit; the blossoming vines spread their fragrance.*
>
> —Song of Songs 2:11-13

Jesus taught in parables using illustrations in nature to convey moral principles. All of us are familiar with the stories about the sower, the mustard seed and the fig tree. When teaching a lesson on anxiety Christ said,

> *Look at the birds of the air; they do not sow or reap or store away in barns, and yet your heavenly Father feeds them. Are you not much more valuable than they? And why do you worry about clothes? See how the lilies of the field grow. They do not labor or spin. Yet I tell you that not even Solomon in all his splendor was dressed like one of these.*
>
> —Matthew 6:26, 28, 29

God's handiwork provides serenity when we need to get away from it all. Garden walks and nature trails supply us with calmness and inner peace, and if you have ever experienced a time when a small child brought you a weed, violet or dandelion from the yard then you were awarded a serendipity.

There is a saying, "Take time to smell the roses." The next time you stop to smell the roses, be sure to look for bunnies.

ABANDONED

I no longer enjoy reading the newspapers or listening to newscasts. In addition to crimes of every nature and the tragedies in relationship to floods, earthquakes, hurricanes, there is more often than not a story of abandonment.

Precisely, what does the word abandon mean? To give up completely; to withdraw protection, support or help; desert; forsake. What an awful word! What a terrible act!

One parent or both leave small children in a house alone with little or no food and do not return for days or weeks. Fathers run away from their responsibilities and desert their families; mothers do the same thing. Unwed girls leave their newborns in restrooms, bus stations, doorsteps and even garbage cans. Others give their babies up for adoption and often in later years regret their decision. Even though some of these families are reunited and all seems to be forgiven, the taint of abandonment still lingers.

Does the Bible have much to say about abandonment? More than you might think. After all God did for the Israelites, they soon forgot the deliverance from Egypt and the food delivered to the doors of their tents. They worshipped idols and broke the covenant forsaking God completely.

> *"Why has the Lord done this to the land? Why this fierce, burning anger?" And the answer will be: 'It is because this people abandoned the covenant of the Lord, the God of their fathers, the covenant he made with them when he brought them out of Egypt.'*
> —Deuteronomy 29:24, 25

The Israelites had a short term memory and their faith failed. Over and over again they abandoned God although he bailed them out of their troubles with other nations.

> *But they forgot the Lord their God; so he sold them into the hand of Sisera, the commander of the army of Hazor, and into the hands of the Philistines and the king of Moab, who fought against them. They cried out to the Lord and said, "We have sinned; we have forsaken the Lord and served the Baals and the Ashtoreth. But now deliver us from the hands of our enemies, and we will serve you."*
> —1 Samuel 12:9, 10

Before we travel too far into the Scriptures we must remember the abandonment of Joseph. Because of jealousy which was probably due in part to the coat that Jacob had made for Joseph and the unusual dreams of Joseph, his brothers abandoned him, sold him as a slave and devised a story of deception to tell their father. Each time I read this account as recorded in the 37th chapter of Genesis I can hardly believe the cruelty of these brothers. How did Joseph feel as he was placed in the well? Did he think he would die? As he was led away by the Midianite merchants did Joseph look back in disbelief? I imagine the fear and hurt was almost unbearable.

Now back to the stormy life of the Israelites. After the death of Solomon the tribes of Judah and Benjamin decided to go their separate way under the leadership of Rehoboam, Solomon's son. The remaining tribes appointed Jeroboam as their king; soon their troubles became more numerous.

Even though the kingdom of Judah remained somewhat more faithful to God, there were periods of abandonment.

> Then the prophet Shemaiah came to Rehoboam and to the leaders of Judah who had assembled in Jerusalem for fear of Shishak, and he said to them, "This is what the Lord says, 'You have abandoned me, therefore, I now abandon you to Shishak.'"
> —2 Chronicles 12:5

Once again the people were humbled and sorrowful. God had compassion on them, delivered them from Shishak but they were subject to him in order that the people would learn the difference in serving God and the foreign kings.

Isaiah's message of condemnation of Judah's many sins:

> You have abandoned your people, the house of Jacob. They are full of superstitions from the East: they practice divination like the Philistines and clasp hands with pagans.
> —Isaiah 2:6

The prophets, acting as intermediaries for God, had the awesome responsibility of delivering messages from God which pinpointed their sins.

> O Lord, the hope of Israel, all who forsake you will be put to shame. Those who turn away from you will be written in dust because they have forsaken the Lord, the spring of living water.
> —Jeremiah 17:13

No one felt the sting of abandonment as keenly as our Savior. His disciples who had vowed their loyalty and had partaken of the Last Supper only a few hours before his arrest fled in panic and deserted Him (Matthew 24:56).

Even though the disciples had been closely associated with Jesus, sitting at His feet as he taught and observing first hand the miracles, they fled and deserted Him in His greatest hour of need.

Where could He turn? To whom could He appeal?

From the sixth hour until the ninth hour darkness came over all the land. About the ninth hour Jesus cried out in a loud voice, "Eloi, Eloi, lama sabachthani?"--which means, "My God, my God, why have you forsaken me?"
—Matthew 27:45, 46

Why did God forsake His only Son--the beloved Son in whom He was well pleased? It was necessary because Christ had to bear the cross alone; only He could transport the sins of the world to Himself so that we could be free from sin.

God cannot be in the presence of sin; He had to turn His back during that dreadful hour. I don't believe that we as humans can possibly imagine the agony of Jesus. In addition to excruciating pain He had to endure the torture of being abandoned by everyone--everyone, even His Father.

What is the message for us? We may not be guilty of forsaking families or friends but do we at times, unknowingly, forsake our Savior? Are we so busy with the affairs of this world that we fail to put Christ first in our lives? Maybe Satan has crept up on us unawares and through neglect and apathy we have become less faithful.

We need to take inventory often to make certain that we do not become guilty of abandoning God. He will never forsake us if we remain faithful, and even when we stumble now and then, He is ready and willing to forgive if we are penitent. This the glory of the cross.

Those who know your name will trust in you, for you, Lord, have never forsaken those who seek you.
—Psalm 9:10

72

ANGELS AWAIT

Do not forget to entertain [show love to] strangers, for by so doing some people have entertained angels without knowing it.
—Hebrews 13:2

Who are they? What do they do, and under whose authority? How much power do they have and how much do they know? Numerous questions come to mind as we think about angels. Books have been written, television programs dramatize encounters with them, and yet how much do we really know and how much of this information is authentic?

Being the curious person that I am, I have thought for some time that I would like to make an in-depth study of angelogy—but dare I delve into the deeps to the point that I would feel comfortable in writing about this intriguing subject? I can't resist—so with several Bibles at hand, commentaries and *The New Strong's Exhaustive Concordance of the Bible* at hand I have launched a study that has taken more time than any other but it has been intensely interesting and rewarding. I hope you will find the same thing to be true.

I'm not going to second-guess, make suppositions or form opinions. The material is being presented exactly as it appears in the Holy Word. *Strong's Concordance* has over 200 listings for the word "angel" and more than 75 for the plural "angels." Noting this many references almost made me faint-hearted—almost.

First we need a definition of angels. They are celestial (heavenly) beings superior to man (in some respects) created by God to be His agents and messengers to carry out His orders.

He [Christ] is the image of the invisible God, the firstborn over all creation. For by him all things were created: things in heaven and on earth, visible and invisible, whether thrones or powers or rulers or authorities; all things were created by and for him.
—Colossians 1:15, 16

There are angels of light and there are angels of darkness; angels of God and angels of Satan.

And there was war in heaven. Michael and his angels fought against the dragon, and the dragon and his angels fought back. But he was not strong enough, and they lost their place in heaven. The great dragon was hurled down—that ancient serpent called the devil, or

73

Satan, who leads the whole world astray. He was hurled to the earth, and his angels with him.

—Revelation 12:7-9

We know that Christ is the Prince of peace and Prince of the kingdom of God, but until this world ends Satan is the prince of this world. He and his angels of darkness continue to carry out their diabolical deeds as they wait to ensnare us when we are weak or have let down our guard.

God did not spare angels when they sinned, but sent them to hell, putting them into gloomy dungeons to be held for judgment.
—2 Peter 2:4

Let's concentrate on the angels of God and hopefully learn more about them. They are not omnipotent, omnipresent or omniscient, but are given special powers by God to carry out His commands. We know that they can appear as human beings because we have numerous references about unusual events when angels were disguised as humans.

In the 18th chapter of Genesis we read the fascinating story of Abraham being visited by three men. One of these men revealed himself as the Lord and told Abraham that he would have a son by Sarah.

After God gave the Ten Commandments and other laws regarding justice and mercy, He said this to the people,

"See, I am sending an angel ahead of you to guard you along the way and to bring you to the place I have prepared. Pay attention to him and listen to what he says. Do not rebel against him; for he will not forgive your rebellion since my Name is in him."
—Exodus 23:20, 21

Do we have any reason to believe that God no longer sends His angels to help us? I think not.

The angel of the Lord encamps around those who fear him, and he delivers them.
—Psalm 34:7

If you make the Most High your dwelling—even the Lord, who is my refuge—then no harm will befall you, no disaster will come near

74

your tent. For he will command his angels concerning you to guard you in all your ways; they will lift you up in their hands, so that you will not strike your foot against a stone.
                                                              —Psalm 91:9-12

Can we ever forget the events in the life of Daniel regarding angels? As children we loved the stories of the fiery furnace and the den of lions, and we were fascinated when the teacher pronounced the names of Shadrach, Meshach and Abednego. Three men were thrown into the furnace but a fourth person was seen walking around with them—the angel of the Lord sent to protect them.

Daniel was thrown into the den of lions because he had violated a decree of King Darius. Daniel held a high position at this time and was highly favored by Darius but the king was left with no other choice. Darius was unable to eat or sleep as a result of this action but by dawn the scene had changed.

At the first light of dawn, the king got up and hurried to the lions' den. When he came near the den, he called to Daniel in an anguished voice, "Daniel, servant of the living God, has your God, whom you serve continually, been able to rescue you from the lions?" Daniel answered, "O king, live forever! My God sent his angel, and he shut the mouths of the lions. They have not hurt me, because I was found innocent in his sight."
                                                              —Daniel 6:19-22

At God's bidding angels can take on human forms and at times characteristics of the elements.

In speaking of the angels he says, "He makes his angels winds, his servants flames of fire."
                                                              —Hebrews 1:7

An angel brought Zechariah the news that he would have a son—John the Baptist.

An angel of the Lord appeared to Zechariah, standing at the right side of the altar of incense. When Zechariah saw him, he was startled and was gripped with fear. But the angel said to him:

"Do not be afraid, Zechariah; your prayer has been heard. Your wife Elizabeth will bear you a son, and you are to give him the name John."
                                                              —Luke 1:13

75

Angels have names; we are familiar with Gabriel and Michael. They are archangels which means they have a higher rank. Gabriel was sent to Mary to announce the birth of Jesus, and his appearance was troubling to her at first.

> The angel went to her and said, "Greetings, you who are highly fa-vored! The Lord is with you." Mary was greatly troubled at his words and wondered what kind of greeting this might be. But the angel said to her, "Do not be afraid, Mary, you have found favor with God. You will be with child and give birth to a son, and you are to give him the name Jesus. He will be great and will be called the Son of the Most High. The Lord God will give him the throne of his father David, and he will reign over the house of Jacob forever; his kingdom will never end."
>
> —Luke 1:28-33

What form did Gabriel take when he appeared to Mary? Was he in human form or did he have a heavenly appearance, such as a halo or glow? The Bible does not say, but the fact that Mary was fear-ful denotes that this was an unusual event. Later God sent His angel to console Joseph and affirmed that the baby Mary was to have would indeed by the Savior.

Angels appeared again at the birth of Jesus. While shepherds were watching their flocks at night an angel of the Lord appeared to them and the scriptures say that the glory of the Lord shone around them, so much that the shepherds were terrified.

> But the angel said to them, "Do not be afraid. I bring you good news of great joy that will be for all the people. Today in the town of David a Savior has been born to you; he is Christ the Lord. This will be a sign to you: You will find a baby wrapped in cloths and lying in a manger." Suddenly a great company of the heavenly host appeared with the angel praising God and saying, "Glory to God in the high-est, and on earth peace to men on whom his favor rests."
>
> —Luke 2:10-14

After Jesus fasted for forty days and Satan tempted Him, an-gels attended Him. Did they bring Him food? What exactly did they do? We don't know—the Word just says the angels ministered to Him.

At the empty tomb on resurrection day we encounter an angel. This time he is described as a young man dressed in a white robe sit-ting on the right side. Naturally the women were alarmed, but he tells them of the glorious resurrection and instructs them to go and tell the disciples and Peter.

Now we come to a scripture that may be a little difficult to understand. Jesus has just informed His disciples that unless they become like little children they will never enter the kingdom of heaven. In answer to their question as to who is the greatest in the kingdom of heaven, He tells them that whoever humbles himself like the little child standing before them is the greatest in the kingdom of heaven. Now the passage:

> *See that you do not look down on one of these little ones. For I tell you that their angels in heaven always see the face of my Father in heaven.*
>
> —Matthew 18:10

Does this not say that little children have representatives (angels) at God's throne? We know that we must become like little children (that is, humble) and when we do so, are there angels at the throne of God representing us? I'll let you think about it and decide because I said at the beginning I would not express my opinion.

Let's take a visual journey with Paul as he sails for Rome. Paul and some other prisoners are aboard ship when a storm arises. The wind was so fierce that they were set adrift and it became necessary for them to throw the cargo overboard. They had gone a long time without food and the situation seemed bleak and desperate when Paul speaks:

> *But now I urge you to keep up your courage, because not one of you will be lost; only the ship will be destroyed. Last night an angel of the God whose I am and whom I serve stood beside me and said, "Do not be afraid, Paul. You must stand trial before Caesar; and God has graciously given you the lives of all who sail with you."*
>
> —Acts 27:22-24

Let's note a few more scriptures regarding angels. Jesus was teaching the parable of the lost coin, stating how the woman and neighbors rejoiced when the coin was found.

> *In the same way, I tell you, there is rejoicing in the presence of the angels of God over one sinner who repents.*
>
> —Luke 15:10

The time was when the apostles were put in jail by the Sadducees because of jealousy.

> *But during the night an angel of the Lord opened the doors of the jail and brought them out.*
>
> —Acts 5:19

A very comforting passage is found in the first chapter of Hebrews, 14th verse:

> *Are not all angels ministering spirits sent to serve those who will inherit salvation?*

We don't know exactly the manner in which angels minister to us, but because they are the servants and agents of God we can be certain that they still have duties. It is questionable whether each child of God has a particular guardian angel, but the Bible does confirm that when we ask God for help, strength, comfort that He helps us. The means by which this is done could very well be by angels although we are unaware of their presence.

Angels surround God's throne and await His bidding to carry out the missions God has for them. They cannot make decisions but are faithful in their duties, and at the time of death they come and carry the souls of saints on wings as they fly away home.

Isn't it wonderful to contemplate that angels will bear our souls on their wings and transport us from this world of pain, sorrow, heartache and turmoil to the heavenly realms into the presence of God?

> *When the Son of Man comes in his glory, and all the angels with him, he will sit on his throne in heavenly glory.*
>
> —Matthew 25:31

P.S. I want to leave this topic with an interesting scripture.

> *Do you not know that we will judge angels?*
>
> —1 Corinthians 6:3

IMPETUOUS—UNDAUNTED

All of us, at times, have said and done things impulsively and immediately wished we could take back the words and undo the deeds. Some people by nature always run ahead without thinking; others make snap judgments and jump to conclusions.

Did Sarai act on impulse when she decided to give Hagar to Abram, or did she give it some thought? In either case she did not wait on the Lord and the results of her action brought many sorrows and repercussions even to the present time.

Moses, in frustration, acted impulsively when he struck the rock to bring forth water although God had told him to speak to the rock.

God's command to Moses:

Take the staff, and you and your brother Aaron gather the assembly together. Speak to that rock before their eyes and it will pour out its water. You will bring water out of the rock for the community so they and their livestock can drink.
—Numbers 20:8

Then Moses raised his arm and struck the rock twice with his staff. Water gushed out, and the community and their livestock drank. But the Lord said to Moses and Aaron, "Because you did not trust in me enough to honor me as holy in the sight of the Israelites, you will not bring this community into the land I give them."
—Numbers 20:11, 12

Moses paid a high price for this sin--God did not permit him to enter the promised land, but undaunted he continued to lead the Israelites and passed authority to Joshua.

Moses came with Joshua son of Nun and spoke all the words of this song in the hearing of the people. When Moses finished reciting all these words to all Israel, he said to them, "Take to heart all the words I have solemnly declared to you this day, so that you may command your children to obey carefully all the words of this law. They are not just idle words for you--they are your life. By them you will live long in the land you are crossing the Jordan to possess."
—Deuteronomy 32:44-47

Daniel is a good example of being undaunted even in the face of danger--perhaps death. He was committed to his God and refused to eat the king's food although he was a captive in Babylon.

But Daniel resolved not to defile himself with the royal food and wine, and he asked the chief official for permission not to defile himself this way.

—Daniel 1:8

Again, fearlessly, Daniel defied the king's decree to pray only to him. If you had been Daniel what would you have done? Could you, could I, have been so brave and so faithful to God knowing that we might lose our lives? Aren't you glad that we do not face this situation? But sometimes I wonder if maybe we fail the test and do not stand firm, undaunted, in our conviction.

Now when Daniel learned that the decree had been published, he went home to his upstairs room where the windows opened toward Jerusalem. Three times a day he got down on his knees and prayed, giving thanks to his God, just as he had done before.

—Daniel 6:10

You know the rest of this story--how he was thrown into the den of lions and God sent an angel during the night to shut the lions' mouths.

We will not be threatened by a den of lions, or a fiery furnace, but we probably will be confronted by an angel of darkness who will tempt us in various ways to be less faithful.

Who is the next character that comes to mind? If you said, "Peter," you're right. No person in the New Testament was as head strong, bold, impulsive, and daring as was Peter. He made mistakes over and over again because of his impulsiveness but he remained undaunted.

Walking on water! What a scene! I can't imagine, can you, what a magnificent spectacle to witness as Jesus walks offshore towards the boat occupied by the disciples? At first they thought He was a ghost but then He called to them:

Take courage! It is I. Don't be afraid. "Lord, if it's you," Peter replied, "tell me to come to you on the water." "Come," he said.

—Matthew 14:27-29

What did the other disciples think as they saw impetuous Peter leave the boat in turbulent winds to walk on water to the waiting Savior?

Then Peter got down out of the boat, walked on the water and came toward Jesus. But when he saw the wind, he was afraid and beginning to sink, cried out, "Lord, save me!" Immediately Jesus reached out his hand and caught him. "You of little faith," he said, "why did you doubt?'

Peter's faith faltered and failed in an impulsive moment. Can we identify with this impetuousness? Mistakes and failures are often the results of such actions. But, undaunted, Peter continued.

After six days Jesus took with him Peter, James and John the brother of James, and led them up a high mountain by themselves. There he was transfigured before them. His face shone like the sun, and his clothes became as white as the light. Just then there appeared before them Moses and Elijah, talking with Jesus. Peter said to Jesus, "Lord, it is good for us to be here. If you wish, I will put up three shelters--one for you, one for Moses and one for Elijah." While he was still speaking, a bright cloud enveloped them, and a voice from the cloud said, "This is my Son, whom I Love; with him I am well pleased. Listen to him!"
—Matthew 17:1-5

Once again, without thinking, Peter has made a suggestion that was inappropriate and unwise. Nevertheless, it appears that he continued undaunted.

Peter was like some of us--wanting to be first on the scene, the first to make suggestions, and many of these things backfire. But, probably, the greatest regret and sorrow of Peter's life was his denial of his Lord.

Peter replied, "Even if all fall away on account of you I never will." "I tell you the truth," Jesus answered, "this very night, before the rooster crows, you will disown me three times." But Peter declared, "Even if I have to die with you, I will never disown you."
—Matthew 26:33-35

A short time later Peter did what he had adamantly said he would not do--even cursing--he denied three times that he knew Jesus. I cannot imagine the heartache that overtook Peter as to rooster crowed.

And he went outside and wept bitterly.

—Matthew 26:75

I think I would have left town, feeling that I could never face my Savior again, but Peter after repenting in bitter tears carried on undaunted.

We find Peter next at the tomb of Jesus. On the first day of the week Mary Magdalene, Mary the mother of James and Salome brought spices to the tomb to anoint the body of Jesus. When they entered they were met by a young man dressed in white who told them Christ had risen and was not there.

But go, tell his disciples and Peter, "He is going ahead of you into Galilee. There you will see him, just as he told you."

—Mark 16:7

Why was Peter singled out? Why did the angel say to tell the disciples AND Peter? Did the denial have a bearing on this statement, or the fact that he was always so impetuous? I think that Jesus knowing the anguish and sorrow engulfing Peter, was letting him know that He forgave him, and that he was still a member of the inner circle and a disciple. What do you think?

The disciples did not believe the report of the women but Luke says that Peter got up and ran to the tomb and saw the strips of linen and he went away wondering. John's account is very interesting:

So Peter and the other disciple (John) started for the tomb. Both were running, but the other disciple outran Peter and reached the tomb first. He bent over and looked in at the strips of linen lying there but did not go in. Then Simon Peter, who was behind him, arrived and went into the tomb. He saw the strips of linen lying there, as well as the burial cloth that had been around Jesus' head_.

—John 20:3-7

Let's look in on one more scene after Christ's resurrection. The disciples have gone fishing and have not caught anything. Jesus is standing on shore and called to them but they do not recognize him. He called out to them, "Friends, haven't you any fish?" "No," they answered. Jesus tells them to throw the net on the right side of the boat. They caught so many fish they were unable to haul them in.

Then the disciple whom Jesus loved said to Peter, "It is the Lord!" As soon as Simon Peter heard him say, "It is the Lord," he wrapped his outer garment around him (for he had taken it off) and jumped into the water.

—John 21:7

Peter once again displays his impetuous nature as he jumps into the water and goes ashore to Jesus. An event follows that I think we don't read often or concentrate on. When the disciples come ashore they find that Jesus has started a fire and He is cooking fish and bread. Jesus not only performs a miracle regarding the catch of fish but cooks and serves breakfast to His disciples. What an emotional experience! It was only a brief period of time since the mock trial and the cruel death of the cross; only a few weeks since the glorious resurrection, and yet Christ prepares a simple breakfast to serve his disciples. He knows He is leaving soon and they will be on their own. What will the disciples do--what will Peter do?

Following the breakfast Jesus has a conversation with Peter in which he reinstates Peter. When Peter affirms his love for Him then Jesus tells him to feed his sheep and take care of his lambs.

I believe Peter was able to forgive himself also, as he went on to many outstanding endeavors. We must forgive ourselves when we make mistakes whether it be a faux pas or something more serious. We know that God forgives us, therefore, we must let go of past false steps and go on undaunted as Peter did.

Peter had the privilege of preaching the first sermon on the day of Pentecost, witnessing the arrival of the Holy Spirit as promised by Christ. He was also responsible for the first Gentile convert, Cornelius. When Jesus was still on earth he had awarded the keys of the kingdom of heaven to Peter because he had confessed Christ as the Son of the living God.

All of us must try not to be impetuous. Think before you speak and act, but when you make mistakes, make amends if possible and carry on undaunted.

LURKING ANGELS

In a previous chapter we talked about angels of light—God's angels—how they surround His throne awaiting His bidding to carry out His missions and purposes. It is very comforting to know that we, as God's children, have the assurance that we will be comforted and aided by whatever means He chooses to use.

Unfortunately, there is a flip side to this. Lurking in unexpected places and times are the angels of darkness, Satan's henchmen as it were, making every effort to entice, ensnare and enslave us. Paul's discourse on forgiveness for the sinner:

> *If you forgive anyone, I also forgive him. And what I have forgiven—if there was anything to forgive—I have forgiven in the sight of Christ for your sake, in order that Satan might not outwit us. For we are not unaware of his schemes.*
> —2 Corinthians 2:10, 11

Satan does not procrastinate, never lets up, never gives up, and when we let down our guard he is ready to send his angels to attack us. He is not only busy in Los Angeles, New Orleans, New York and Washington but in every city, town and hamlet in the world.

The Corinthian letter warns of false apostles and Paul writes the following admonition:

> *For such men are false prophets, deceitful workmen, masquerading as apostles of Christ. And no wonder, for Satan himself masquerades as an angel of light. It is not surprising, then, if his servants masquerade as servants of righteousness. Their end will be what their actions deserve.*
> 2 Corinthians 11:13-15

We are tempted in different ways at different times in our lives. The temptations of youth are not the same as middle age or old age. A young woman may be tempted by the attentions of an attractive young man and eventually succumbs to an illicit encounter. One brief moment can bring a lifetime of regret and heartache.

Young men are often tempted by sparkling wine or glistening beer not realizing that a small amount may result in addiction to perhaps a point of no return. Satan is the mastermind of the drug culture so prevalent today. In an effort to escape reality or thinking that drugs will enhance the mind and body, many have fallen into the death trap of hallucinations, drifting into a dreamy world that ruins health and wrecks lives.

During the middle years people may have some of the same temptations as the young group but objects of a more subtle nature may draw many into a trap—plenty, pleasure and power. Plenty usually calls for more, leading to greed; leisure time and the activities that go with it lure and entice to the point that the important things of life are forgotten. The power struggle becomes an obsession and may engulf and submerge a person ruining family life and religious life.

As the senior years approach many excuses surface—we're too tired, too old, too sick—this becomes the easy way out of obligations and duties. "Let someone else do it, I've done my part" becomes our excuse and when this happens we are easy prey for Satan and his wicked purposes.

Remember, Satan is after good people—he already has bad people in his camp. The ones who are living only for this world, for gratification of the flesh and material possessions have, perhaps unknowingly, signed a contract with the devil. Hopefully, the forces of good will be able to conquer, and repentance and salvation will take place. We know, assuredly, that in the end God and His angels of light will defeat Satan and his angels.

The Christian battle is an ongoing war between the forces of evil and the forces of good. We must be alert and aware at all times because Satan does not take a vacation.

All of us have been and will be tempted—we may even succumb—to shade the truth and dabble in a bit of deception. The lurking angel convinces us that we are not doing anything wrong.

No temptation has seized you except what is common to man. And God is faithful; he will not let you be tempted beyond what you can bear. But when you are tempted, he will also provide a way out so that you can stand up under it.
—1 Corinthians 10:13

Submit yourselves, then, to God. Resist the devil, and he will flee from you. Come near to God and he will come near to you.
—James 4:7, 8

Be self-controlled and alert. Your enemy the devil prowls around like a roaring lion looking for someone to devour. Resist him, standing firm in the faith.

—1 Peter 5:8, 9

Along many highways we see the warning sign WATCH FOR FALLING ROCKS. On our journey through life we need to heed another admonition—WATCH FOR FALLEN ANGELS.

THE GIFT OF ADOPTION

Did you grow up with biological parents or were you raised by adoptive parents? When I was growing up in the 20's and 30's I had two close friends who were adopted. These girls were told as soon as they were able to understand and the situation never seemed unusual or strange to me.

There were other cases in my small hometown in which the adoptive parents tried to conceal the fact of adoption from friends and also the child. Some may have felt a stigma, a tinge of embarrassment that they were unable to have children of their own, or perhaps fear was a factor, not knowing how people would react or if the child would feel shame and resentment.

Have you ever wondered, as I have, why many Christian couples are unable to have children when the world is full of people who do not want children and cannot provide for them?

Each year due to various circumstances thousands of children are left without biological parents to care for them. Some are abandoned, some are left homeless by death; in some cases these children have been neglected, even abused.

Fortunate are those who are adopted by loving, caring people who take them into their homes to be raised, nurtured, educated and loved with all the rights and privileges as if they had been born into the family.

Not everyone is suited to be an adoptive parent—it takes very special people to assume this role. Maybe some couples who are unable to have children biologically are the very ones who possess those special qualities needed to raise the children who have been deprived.

Many times it takes several years for an adoption to go through. Some couples become discouraged, ready to give up at times, but probably this time is needed to better prepare for the task. God has His own timetable and we must wait and be patient for the many things that we desire. God knows when the time is right—we don't.

Finally, the day arrives when the tiny baby is placed in the new adoptive mother's arms, or maybe it is an older child. In some cases the couple decides to take a brother and a sister so that they will not have to be separated. I imagine the feeling is overwhelming as the new parents with compassion and love accept this worthy responsibility.

In fear and trembling and at the same time with joyous anticipation they begin this new journey, willing to make sacrifices so that the child will be educated, trained in Christian virtues, always providing security and a sense of belonging. The parents will give selflessly of time, energy and money.

In return these children have the obligation and responsibility of respecting, loving and obeying the parents. In gratitude they should do their best in all areas of life.

Now I'll ask the question again. Are you an adopted child? If you say, "No," think again. Are you a baptized believer? Have you accepted Christ as your Savior, Guide and King? Are you in complete submission to God? Are you willing to conform to His will for your life? If the answer is "Yes" then what is your status?

> *The Spirit himself testifies with our spirit that we are God's children. Now if we are children, then we are heirs—heirs of God and co-heirs with Christ, if indeed we share in his sufferings in order that we may also share in his glory.*
>
> —Romans 8:16, 17

> *But we ourselves, who have the firstfruits of the Spirit, groan inwardly as we wait eagerly for our adoption as sons, the redemption of our bodies. For those God foreknew he also predestined to be conformed to the likeness of his Son, that he might be the firstborn among many brothers.*
>
> —Romans 8:23, 29

> *But when the time had fully come, God sent his Son, born of a woman, born under law, to redeem those under law, that we might receive the full rights of sons. Because you are sons, God sent the Spirit of his Son into our hearts, the Spirit who calls out, "Abba, Father." So you are no longer a slave, but a son; and since you are a son, God has made you also an heir.*
>
> —Galatians 4:4-7

> *For he chose us in him before the creation of the world to be holy and blameless in his sight. In love he predestined us to be adopted as his sons through Jesus Christ, in accordance with his pleasure and will—to the praise of his glorious grace, which he has freely given us in the One he loves.*
>
> —Ephesians 1:4-6

ISN'T THIS A MARVELOUS CONCEPT!

THE CRY OF THE LONELY BIRD

I lie awake; I have become like a bird alone on a roof.
—Psalm 102:7

The wedding is over—everything was perfect. The young couple gaze into each other's eyes with love, anticipation, hopes and dreams. They plan to spend a lifetime together, growing old with happy memories. So, they live happily ever after. Right? Unfortunately, no.

A few months pass and she discovers that she is pregnant. This wasn't supposed to happen yet. They had planned to wait a few years. She tries to conceal her disappointment as she tells her husband. He is shocked and visibly shaken; in his mind's eye he sees all their plans and hopes for the future vanish. His attempt to hide his feelings is a failure.

The days come and go—tensions mount, tempers flare. She is sick and out of shape. Where is the lovely girl he married only a few short months ago?

Shortly after the birth he does not come home one evening. Days later she receives a letter. He cannot face the responsibility and shattered dreams. He has forgotten a part of the ceremony, "for better or for worse."

Another young woman, aging before her time, is left to raise her child alone.

I cry aloud to the Lord; I lift up my voice to the Lord for mercy. I pour out my complaint before him; before him I tell my trouble.
—Psalm 142:1, 2

Answer me when I call to you, O my righteous God. Give me relief from my distress; be merciful to me and hear my prayer.
—Psalm 4:1

They had been married five years. He was established in a career that had brought several promotions. They had built a new house, they had made wise investments. Now it was time—time to start their family. A year passed and nothing happened. Not discouraged, they wait. Two years passed during which time many doctors were consulted but nothing definitive was found. Three years passed and she felt that her biological clock was winding down.

At the suggestion of a friend she made an appointment with a new specialist in town. Imagine the heartbreak when the doctor informed her she would never be able to have a baby. In time she suggested adoption but her husband said no. He wanted a biological child.

The two grew farther apart and within a year they were divorced. He married again very soon and his new wife conceived almost immediately. This was not the way it was supposed to be. Another commitment broken.

In my distress I called to the Lord; I cried to my God for help. From his temple he heard my voice; my cry came before him, into his ears.
—Psalm 18:6

She was talented and beautiful. Her husband was loving, caring, supportive—a good father to their four-year-old daughter. She decided to get a job, to use the skills she had acquired and for fulfillment.

She liked her job and was on the way up "the ladder." The little girl was in preschool and was happy. Everything was going well until the day a new man joined the company. He was attractive, outgoing and ambitious. She was immediately attracted to him and he to her; however, she tried to deny this to herself.

They sat in groups together in the company cafeteria. One day he suggested they go elsewhere for lunch; the cafeteria food was boring and they needed a change, so he said. Harmless enough, maybe but risky. The lunches away from the company cafeteria became more frequent. Then one day when she mentioned that her husband was out of town on business, he suggested a dinner engagement. She hesitated but accepted when she remembered her daughter would be spending the night with a friend.

She had never asked about his marital status. He had never mentioned a family and she felt that he would tell her in due time. He was divorced but gave no details. She didn't ask, perhaps not wanting to know the answer. She and her husband were Christians with strong convictions regarding divorce. Both of them believed in the lifetime commitment—until death parts us. Later that evening when she was home alone, sleep eluded her. A fresh, new excitement swept over her as never before.

Although the lunch dates continued on a regular basis it was several months before they went out in the evening again. This time emotions were strong, the attraction deepening, desire out of control—her marriage vows were broken and lives shattered forever.

Eventually after many efforts on the part of the husband had failed the marriage ended in divorce. She married the other man and did not ask for joint custody of their daughter. Another little girl abandoned by her mother. The father, broken-hearted and distraught, tried the best he could to raise the daughter and give her a good life.

The righteous cry out, and the Lord hears them; he delivers them
from all their troubles. The Lord is close to the brokenhearted and
saves those who are crushed in spirit.
—Psalm 34:17, 18

They had been married over forty years. In their late 60's and early 70's both enjoyed good health. Life was good. The children were gone and established in their homes. Now free from prior responsibilities they were able to travel; however, they never neglected worship and church-related activities, always lending a helping hand to others and involving themselves in good deeds.

One day when least expected, the bubble burst—the man was very ill. In four short months he was gone, a victim of cancer. While still in shock and disbelief the wife realized she did not feel well. A visit to the doctor dealt an almost unbelievable blow. She, too, had cancer.

How could this be? Why did it happen to them? Where could she turn? Her whole world was falling apart. Some women would have given up in despair. Many would have become bitter and cynical, denouncing God, but this woman was made of different material. Her will to fight and live was very strong although she was facing obstacles and hurdles she never dreamed of.

Save me, O God, for the waters have come up to my neck. I sink in
the miry depths, where there is no foothold. I have come into the deep
waters; the floods engulf me. I am worn out calling for help; my
throat is parched.
—Psalm 69:1-3

This woman's fight is not over but she is doing well. With the help of good doctors, family and friends, and the prayers of many, she leads a normal life, still able to help others.

God is our refuge and strength, an ever-present help in trouble.
—Psalm 46:1

O Lord, hear my prayer, listen to my cry for mercy; in your faithfulness and righteousness come to my relief.
—Psalm 143:1

There are more scenes to observe—we are standing near the door of a hospital room. The man is holding the woman's hand; she is pale and drawn as the doctor says, "Your baby did not survive." Across the hall another doctor informs a couple that their child has physical and mental disabilities. The silence is deafening but their hearts are screaming with pain and anguish.

And we rejoice in the hope of the glory of God. Not only so, but we also rejoice in our sufferings, because we know that suffering produces perseverance; perseverance, character; and character, hope. And hope does not disappoint us, because God has poured out his love into our hearts by the Holy Spirit, whom he has given us.
—Romans 5:2b-5

For our light and momentary troubles are achieving for us an eternal glory that far outweighs them all. So we fix our eyes not on what is seen, but on what is unseen. For what is seen is temporary, but what is unseen is eternal.
—2 Corinthians 4:17, 18

Now let's go to the cemetery—family and friends are gathered at the open grave. The lives of two young people in their 20's have been snuffed out in a split second in a speeding vehicle, the result of alcohol.

Another open grave is nearby—the group cannot believe what has happened. A bright teenager with everything going for her; has failed to seek help for the pressures overwhelming her and has committed suicide. The broken hearts of loved ones cry out, "Why? Why?"

So do not fear, for I am with you; do not be dismayed, for I am your God. I will strengthen you and help you; I will uphold you with my righteous right hand.

—Isaiah 41:10

Even though there are many more stories to tell on life's road of sorrow, we will look in on only one more. It is 2 A.M. A light is on in the house; a weary mother is lying on a sofa, drifting in and out of a restless sleep. She is waiting for her teenage son to come home. It is past his curfew. As terrible thoughts run through her mind the phone rings and the voice speaks the words every parent dreads to hear, "Mom, I'm in jail, I've been arrested for speeding and DUI."

These Christian parents had tried so hard to teach their children what is right. They were good examples and had tried to emphasize the importance of making right choices. Where did they go wrong? Who's to blame? What's to blame? There seems to be no answer.

Some people blame God for the bad things that happen to them, but God does not cause them. When the natural laws, which were set in motion at the time of creation, and God's laws are violated, serious consequences must follow.

But what about long, severe illnesses and premature deaths that come to the good as well as the bad? They are a part of this temporary existence, a reminder that we are only traveling through. If everything was perfect in this world we would not desire or look forward to heaven; in fact, we would not be fit subjects for the eternal abode.

Life is a proving ground, a test site. The way we handle our problems, sorrows and illnesses is a window into our inner being—it proves and shows who we really are and what we are. Do we trust God to see us through? Is our faith strong enough?

God created a perfect world but sin and death made an early entrance through the rebellion of Adam and Eve. But God planned a way of escape and provided comfort and help for His obedient children through the gift of the Holy Spirit.

Only when we submit completely to God are we able to survive the sorrows and tribulations that come to all sooner or later. In adversity our perspective changes, reliance on God comes and another route must be taken.

Christian counselors and support groups can be very helpful but our main support system is our heavenly connection.

Cast all your anxiety on him because he cares for you.
—1 Peter 5:7

He heals the brokenhearted and binds up their wounds.
—Psalm 147:3

Come to me, all you who are weary and burdened, and I will give you rest. Take my yoke upon you and learn from me, for I am gentle and humble in heart, and you will find rest for your souls. For my yoke is easy and my burden is light.
—Matthew 11:28-30

Turn to me and be gracious to me, for I am lonely and afflicted. The troubles of my heart have multiplied; free me from my anguish. Look upon my affliction and my distress and take away all my sins.
—Psalm 25:16-18

Though you have made me see troubles, many and bitter, you will restore my life again; from the depths of the earth you will again bring me up. You will increase my honor and comfort me once again.
—Psalm 71:20, 21

BREAKING THE SHACKLES

Hands behind the back, wrists together, the click of the hand-cuffs; feet locked in chains, little mobility, deprived of freedom—trapped like a wild animal. A criminal or even a suspect has to endure this treatment until proven guilty or innocent. If found guilty the prisoner hears the sharp sound as the barred doors close.

The history of mankind is filled with accounts of innocent people being enslaved. When Joseph was sold by his brothers did the Midianites bind him? Was he restrained with a rope so that he couldn't run away? The slavery of Joseph had a special purpose—God's plan to preserve Jacob and his family, and also to teach the great story of forgiveness.

> *Then Joseph said to his brothers, "Come close to me." When they had done so, he said, "I am your brother Joseph, the one you sold into Egypt! And now, do not be distressed and do not be angry with yourselves for selling me here, because it was to save lives that God sent me ahead you."*
>
> —Genesis 45:4, 5

Later after the death of Joseph and his generation a new king came to power who feared the Israelites because they had increased in great numbers.

> *They made their lives bitter with hard labor in brick and mortar and with all kinds of work in the fields; in all their hard labor the Egyptians used them ruthlessly.*
>
> —Exodus 1:14

The Israelites were held hostage in Egypt because of their sins. God often used heathen nations to punish His people for their sins. One would think after being released from the Egyptians and witnessing God's power in the miracles that they would be ready to obey God and be faithful. Not so!

Time and again God's chosen people endured bondage because of rebellion. The warnings of the prophets fell on deaf and defiant ears. As a result the Israelites were enslaved by Assyria, Babylon and Persia. The Babylonian captivity lasted 70 years. You might want to refresh your memory by reading 1 and 2 Kings and 2 Chronicles.

In spite of idolatry and rebellion God had compassion on His people.

> *Though we are slaves, our God has not deserted us in our bondage. He has shown us kindness in the sight of the kings of Persia.*
> —Ezra 9:9

Down through the ages innocent people have been imprisoned—fastened with shackles through no fault of their own— sometimes because of religious beliefs, political affiliations or ethnic backgrounds. The apostles were arrested many times and Paul was a long-term prisoner.

> *It is because of the hope of Israel that I am bound with this chain.*
> —Acts 28:20

> *May the Lord show mercy to the household of Onesiphorus,, because he often refreshed me and was not ashamed of my chains.*
> —2 Timothy 1:16

Our nation was guilty of greed and lacking in compassion when the innocent people of Africa were brought to this country in chains. Ruthless Hitler in his diabolical scheme to annihilate the Jewish people enslaved thousands in concentration camps and committed countless murders. These people suffered not because of what they had done or failed to do but because of who they were.

As terrible as human bondage is, it pales in comparison to spiritual slavery. Until we became Christians (baptized believers) we were held captive by Satan—only through the supreme sacrifice of Christ and our obedience to Him were the shackles of sin removed.

> *But God demonstrates his own love for us in this: While we were still sinners, Christ died for us. Since we have now been justified by his blood, how much more shall we be saved from God's wrath through him!*
> —Romans 5:8, 9

> *In him we have redemption through his blood, the forgiveness of sins, in accordance with the riches of God's grace that he lavished on us with all wisdom and understanding.*
> —Ephesians 1:7, 8

He did not enter by means of the blood of goats and calves; but he entered the Most Holy Place once for all by his own blood, having obtained eternal redemption.
—Hebrews 9:12

With this in mind we're home free now, aren't we? Unfortunately not quite. We are still humans living in a world under Satan's control (up to a point), and we fall into his trap from time to time and are once again bound by chains.

The spiritual battle is an ongoing struggle but with God's help we can overcome if we remain continually vigilant. Satan does not give up on us when we become Christians; he works even harder to entice us through greed, materialism, self-sufficiency, selfishness, indifference, jealousy, pleasure, power, pride and attitude.

Let's zero in on being opinionated and judgmental. We may be holding to traditions and rituals not bound or authorized by God. Within the hallowed halls of church buildings there are those who attempt, sometimes successfully, to bind their opinions and traditions on others. Examples: same time of worship, same order of worship, same songs, same version of the Bible. If you are content with this arrangement, fine, but don't condemn or judge others if they want to do things in a different order always keeping in mind that we must conform to biblical principles.

Although the King James Version of the Bible was the first English translation there are other good versions. It is good to use more than one in reading and studying. We know that the Holy Scriptures are just that—inspired writers guided by the Holy Spirit were led into all righteousness; however, no one particular version is holier than another.

The words "Thee" and "Thou" are no holier than "You" and "Yours." Many of our beautiful old hymns were written in Old English and I enjoy singing them, but there are also many new songs written in contemporary language that are just as beautiful and meaningful.

Do you regard one day more special than another or is every day the same to you?

One man considers one day more sacred than another; another man considers every day alike. Each one should be fully convinced in his own mind. He who regards one day as special, does so to the Lord.
—Romans 14:5, 6

At the one time of the year when all of Christendom thinks about the birth of Jesus why would anyone go to such an extreme of almost refusing to acknowledge His birth at all? This is fear entrenched in the minds of some because we don't know the exact date of Christ's birth and have not been given a command to observe His birthday.

If you don't want to make one day more special than another that's your privilege. If you do want to make one day more special than another you have that right—but don't force your opinion either way on someone else.

It is time to break the shackles that bind us. Whatever the sin is, whether overt or a sin of attitude, by God's grace you can be free— free to praise Him, honor Him, worship Him in spirit and in truth, and walk in His footsteps.

You will be so happy! I know you will—I've been there!

TENDING THE ROSE GARDEN

The rose is considered by many to be the most beautiful and nearly perfect of all the flowers created by God. It has the qualities of elegance, purity, softness and unequalled beauty. Touch—the delicate petal is the ultimate feeling incomparable with any other.

Roses are not easy to grow. Unlike many other flowers that will grow and bloom in any kind of soil and under different conditions, the rose requires special attention. It has to be fed, sprayed, worked and watered in a special way. Roses are subject to insects and diseases requiring applications of proper chemicals. For these reasons many people will not grow them. The desire must be strong enough to put forth the effort, time and energy to produce the finest specimens.

Life's relationships are similar to a rose garden. Whether in the links of marriage, parents and children, or friends or business partnerships, nurturing and cultivation must take place for bonds to be established.

Marriages break down, suffocate and often die due to lack of attention. Marriage is a difficult job—an ongoing process of caring, nurturing, understanding, forgiveness, and compassion.

Courtship is supposed to be a time of learning about each other—the hopes, dreams and goals desired. Many topics should be discussed such as the spiritual welfare of the home, duties and responsibilities of each, and, importantly, how to raise and discipline the children.

Unfortunately, most of these questions go unanswered or not addressed due to the excitement and passion connected to the tangible aspects of a wedding. It is not until later that reality sets in and the mask is removed.

Submit to one another out of reverence for Christ. Wives, submit to your husbands as to the Lord. For the husband is the head of the wife as Christ is the head of the church, his body, of which he is the Savior. Now as the church submits to Christ, so also wives should submit to their husbands in everything. Husbands, love your wives, just as Christ loved the church and gave himself up for her to make her holy, cleansing her by the washing with water through the word, and to present her to himself as a radiant church, without stain or wrinkle or any other blemish, but holy and blameless. In this same way, husbands ought to love their wives as their own bodies. He who

loves his wife loves himself. After all, no one ever hated his own
body, but he feeds and cares for it, just as Christ does the church—
for we are members of his body.

—Ephesians 5:21-30

Children, obey your parents in the Lord, for this is right. "Honor
your father and mother"—which is the first commandment with a
promise—"that it may go well with you and that you may enjoy
long life on the earth." Fathers, do not exasperate your children; in-
stead, bring them up in the training and instruction of the Lord.

—Ephesians 6:1-4

Do nothing out of selfish ambition or vain conceit, but in humility
consider others better than yourselves. Each of you should look not
only to your own interests, but also to the interest of others.

—Philippians 2:3, 4

You, my brothers, were called to be free. But do not use your freedom
to indulge the sinful nature; rather, serve one another in love. The
entire law is summed up in a single command: "Love your neighbor
as yourself."

—Galatians 5:13, 14

So in everything, do to others what you would have them do to you,
for this sums up the Law and the Prophets.

—Matthew 7:12

Just as roses are subject to blackspot and aphids, all human relationships are suppressed by invaders that need to be eradicated.
What are some of the elements that distribute disorder?

1. Absence of COMMUNICATION
2. NEGLECT, failure to devote TIME and ENERGY to the relationship
3. SELFISHNESS—having it my way
4. UNFORGIVING
5. IRRESPONSIBILITY
6. Dearth of UNDERSTANDING
7. Failure to face REALITY
8. Unwilling to APOLOGIZE, not admitting that you have
made a mistake
9. Presence of PRIDE

If communication is not present in the relationship it is
doomed from the beginning. Communication is a two-way street—

100

each person must express his feelings and listen to the feelings of the other person. From this point, we start with the happenings in the early years of marriage.

When the first baby arrives in the home the young couple is overwhelmed with joy. They want this precious child to have the best of everything. Sometimes their unfulfilled hopes and dreams are transferred to the child and unknowingly they may begin to live vicariously through him or her.

An unrealistic desire to shield children from the hurts and harms of life will produce dysfunctional adults resulting in irresponsibility and maladjustments. Giving children everything they ask for, permitting them to have their own way, and emphasizing material values creates selfish, arrogant and disobedient children.

Christ is no longer the center of the home in many cases. The spiritual aspects have been neglected and set aside, replaced by worldly things. Christian homes are being invaded by Satan in a sly, crafty manner as he is so very capable of doing.

As the children get older and participate in many sports and extra-curricular activities, home life is disrupted. Meals are eaten on the run and seldom does the family have a quiet, uninterrupted meal together. If everyone does manage to sit down together at the same time, the television should be turned off and the answering machine turned on.

Devotionals and spiritual nurturing are nonexistent. No wonder homes are disintegrating. Too often the fathers are no longer taking the responsibility and duty of leadership in the home. Their divine obligation is to be the spiritual leader as well as to set the tone for the moral values and guide lines for discipline.

He who brings trouble on his family will inherit only wind, and the fool will be servant to the wise.
—Proverbs 11:29

When fathers fail in their God-given duties children will become disobedient and disrespectful. Soon lives are in turmoil and chaos and homes are shattered.

Wives are not exempt from blame in many instances. Women may become so involved with careers that they neglect the children and their duties in the home. A woman can be so wrapped up in her outside work that she is too tired at night to prepare good meals and give the love and care needed for the family.

BUT, many women, out of necessity, have worked and managed to maintain a stable home life without sacrificing time and values due the family. It is difficult to do this but with cooperation from all of the family members it can be done.

In the discipline of children many parents make the mistake of saying, "Here's a list of things we don't do. You say, 'No,' because we said so." This is an arrogant attitude that will foster rebellion and, most importantly, leaves God out.

Children have the right to know why the family has certain values. They need to learn at an early age that God is the central figure in the home and in their lives. Even a small child will understand if we say, "God is not pleased or happy when you act this way."

> *Fathers, do not exasperate your children; instead, bring them up in the training and instruction of the Lord.*
> —Ephesians 6:4

When Moses gave instructions in the law and the Ten Commandments, he also set forth lessons for the discipline of children.

> *These commandments that I give you today are to be upon your hearts. Impress them on your children. Talk about them when you sit at home and when you walk along the road, when you lie down and when you get up.*
> —Deuteronomy 6:6, 7

Children are required to obey their parents and it will be easier for them to comply when they understand that the parents are also under the authority of God and His word.

None of us is perfect, but we can strive toward perfection as we mature.

> *Therefore let us leave the elementary teachings about Christ and go on to maturity.*
> —Hebrews 6:1

FRIENDSHIP—what a beautiful word! When you say it a feeling of warmth, joy and peace floods the soul. True friendships are rare as they, like all relationships, must be cultivated and nurtured. Just like the beautiful, perfect rose with its fragrance and soft petals, friendships must be watered, cultivated, sprayed and maintained.

102

What causes friendships to wane, die and shatter into broken pieces—sometimesbeyond repair? The same ingredients that cause other human relationships to disintegrate—mainly pride, lack of communication, misunderstandings.

When pride comes, then comes disgrace, but with humility comes wisdom.
—Proverbs 11:2

A man of many companions may come to ruin, but there is a friend who sticks closer than a brother.
—Proverbs 18:24

I'd like to bring some laughter into the heart of you,
Some joy you would remember in everything you do.
I'd like to bring some dreaming to touch the soul of you,
Some magical reminder of friendship hours that flew.
I'd like to bring some comfort when eyes are dimmed with tears,
For life has many phases across a span of years.
I'd like to bring these tokens and lay them at your feet
And add my heart's devotion to make it all complete.
—Hilda Butler Farr

A loyal, unpretentious friend is such a rare and unique blend
Of kindness, patience, tenderness, or truth, and love, and thought-
fulness.
A friend is light where'er you grope,
In darkness, a bright torch of hope.
An unsung, take-for-granted friend is true and faithful to the end.
A friend shares joys when sun shines through and stays when storm
clouds veil the blue.
A friend will wipe away your tears and hug you close to quiet fears.
—Lois Hurst Beattie

Troubled relationships may be salvaged if warning signals are recognized and if obstacles are eradicated. When too much time has passed and too many barriers erected an impasse may be unavoidable—a point of no return compulsory.

Is there a way to avoid the pitfalls of life?

Make sure you are tending the rose garden.

THE PITFALL OF PRIDE

Can you imagine how terrible it would be to fall into a pit? We are familiar with the horror stories of children falling into wells or holes, trapped and unable to get out. We have seen pictures of panic-stricken parents standing by as a rescue unit works endlessly to free the victims.

As terrible as these events are, it is possible to fall into a pit more deadly than a deep hole in the ground. Satan never sleeps; he never stops his evil work. If he is unable to entice us in the more obvious areas he tries another. One of the most insidious ways is through pride.

> *So, if you think you are standing firm, be careful that you don't fall!*
> —1 Corinthians 10:12

What is the exact meaning of "pride" and how does it manifest itself? The word "pride" can have a positive meaning but primarily it is a negative word. We take pride in our children's achievements when they excel in different areas; perhaps we should say we are happy that they want to use their ability and do well.

The words "pride" and "proud" appear forty-eight times in the Scriptures and always in a negative connotation. This would indicate that God is warning us of the pitfall of pride.

First, let's look at the word "humble," the exact opposite of pride.

> *For whoever exalts himself will be humbled, and whoever humbles himself will be exalted.*
> —Matthew 23:12

> *Humble yourselves before the Lord, and he will lift you up.*
> —James 4:10

> *Therefore, whoever humbles himself like this child is the greatest in the kingdom of heaven.*
> —Matthew 18:4

Humility is not a sign of weakness. Rather, it is an indication of the desire to put others first instead of being self-centered and egotistic.

*When pride comes, then comes disgrace, but with humility comes
wisdom.*
—Proverbs 11:2

*A man's pride brings him low, but a man of lowly spirit gains
honor.*
—Proverbs 29:22

People who have been overcome by pride feel self-sufficient
and fail to admit inadequacies. They think they have all the right answers and would never admit a mistake.

Pride prevents one from sharing troubles and hurts of all
kinds—the excuse being that they don't want to burden others. In
truth they are denying reality, unwilling to admit they need help
and support.

*Pride only breeds quarrels, but wisdom is found in those who take
advice.*
—Proverbs 13:10

Pride leads to arrogance and God condemns it.

To fear the Lord is to hate evil; I hate pride and arrogance.
—Proverbs 8:13

Pride goes before destruction, a haughty spirit before a fall.
—Proverbs 16:18

Church leaders are not always exempt from the sin of pride. In
their positions of authority they become conceited and assume they
have all the right answers. For this reason God gave the following
qualification for elders:

*Not a novice, lest being lifted up with pride he fall into the condem-
nation of the devil.*
—1 Timothy 3:6 (KJV)

We must be aware at all times that Satan is just one step behind
us striving to tempt us in ways we would never think possible. We
work diligently to maintain purity in our lives and in religion, but
pride is a deadly sin that may slip up on us.

We dare not risk the possibility of falling into the pit of pride.
Don't be complacent and think that you are immune. The devil

works the hardest among good, faithful Christians; he already has evil people in his camp.

Read your Bible regularly—constantly. Pray without ceasing asking God to give you strength, courage and wisdom to see the warning signs so that you will not fall into the pit of pride.

ARE YOU LISTENING?

The amazing stories of people who have overcome handicaps are an inspiration to me—those who have learned to walk or run again even though doctors and therapists have said otherwise.

I watched the Special Olympics in awe and admiration for these people who have the desire, determination and will to accomplish that which is almost impossible.

The victims of paralysis who use a paint brush held firmly with their teeth and paint beautiful pictures astound me. Some of these people even hold their brush with their toes.

The many accounts of courage and tenacity are captivating but there is one that in several ways surpasses them all—the life of Helen Keller! Can you imagine being blind and deaf, unable to see, hear or speak? As a young child she was like a wild animal, uncontrollable and unteachable, but it was not to remain so.

A caring, compassionate and challenged teacher believed the impossible was possible and was able to release the shackles that bound this young girl. Eventually she not only learned to read, write and speak but became famous the world over as a lecturer and writer.

I thank God for my handicaps; for, through them, I have found myself, my work, and my God.
—Helen Keller

What was the main ingredient necessary for Helen to understand? It was listening. How could she listen if she could not hear? She listened by touch as the water was pumped over her hand and as Anne Sullivan wrote the word "water" in her hand. Helen listened with her heart and touch.

In today's world no one seems to be listening. Warring countries are not listening to each other. Instead they're fighting and killing. Families are not listening—husbands and wives don't communicate. Children don't listen to parents or teachers. Parents don't listen to their children. A cry for help goes unheeded and the result is involvement in drugs, alcohol, sex, crime and suicide. Marriages are broken because someone did not listen, sometimes the husband or sometimes the wife.

107

Yes, these people can hear but they're not listening: "I'm too tired; I'm too busy; it's just kid stuff; I've heard it before; you're nagging again." Other reasons for not listening are fear of reality, unwillingness to accept responsibility and selfishness.

Worst of all, our world is not listening to God.

Therefore consider carefully how you listen. Whoever has will be given more; whoever does not have, even what he thinks he has will be taken from him.

—Luke 8:18
(a parable of Jesus)

Christians who read the Bible regularly, even daily, can quote scriptures word for word but they're not listening.

We must pay careful attention, therefore, to what we have heard, so that we do not drift away.

—Hebrews 2:1

What is the difference between hearing and listening? The first is passive, the second is active. Not everyone is listening in Bible classes and in the worship assembly—they're tired, sick, worrying about troubles in the family; children are disobedient, rebellious; husbands and wives are shouting at each other or maybe completely silent—no communication.

Life is difficult and many times seems to be coming apart at the seams, but often the complications are the result of non-communication—not listening.

In recent years I have heard several preachers say, "We must get back to the open Bible; not relying on what someone said many years ago or yesterday." This is a good admonition, but unless we listen as we read the open Bible we are still in a stagnant position.

And we have the word of the prophets made more certain, and you will do well to pay attention to it, as to a light shining in a dark place, until the day dawns and the morning star rises in your hearts.
—2 Peter 1:19

The starting point is found in Mark 12:29-31 when a teacher of the law came to Jesus and asked Him, "Of all the commandments, which is the most important?"

"The most important one," answered Jesus, "is this: 'Hear, O Israel, the Lord, our God, the Lord is one. Love the Lord your God with all your heart and with all your soul and with all your mind and with all your strength.' The second is this: 'Love your neighbor as yourself.' There is no commandment greater than these."

When we love God in this manner we will hear, listen, pay attention and act accordingly. This scripture is the basis of a cure for all the ills of mankind.

Family life as it should be is almost a thing of the past. Too many activities interfere with family togetherness; families seldom share a meal.

Be devoted to one another in brotherly love. Honor one another above yourselves.
—Romans 12:10

Do nothing out of selfish ambition or vain conceit, but in humility consider others better than yourselves. Each of you should look not only to your own interests, but also to the interests of others.
—Philippians 2:3, 4

Husbands need to listen to their wives and wives to their husbands. Children need to be heard because each family member has inadequacies that require attention.

Wives, submit to your husbands as to the Lord. For the husband is the head of the wife as Christ is the head of the church, his body, of which he is the Savior. Now as the church submits to Christ, so also wives should submit to their husbands in everything. Husbands, love your wives, just as Christ loved the church and gave himself up for her to make her holy, cleansing her by the washing with water through the word, and to present her to himself as a radiant church, without stain or wrinkle or any other blemish, but holy and blameless. In this same way, husbands ought to love their wives as their own bodies. He who loves his wife loves himself. After all, no one ever hated his own body, but he feeds and cares for it, just as Christ does the church—for we are members of his body.
—Ephesians 5:22-30

It is imperative that parents listen to their children and pay attention to their cries for help which may not be audible but indicated by silent signals.

*Fathers, do not exasperate your children; instead, bring them up in
the training and instruction of the Lord.*
—Ephesians 6:4

Children, also, are instructed to listen:

*Children, obey your parents in the Lord, for this is right. "Honor
your father and mother"—which is the first commandment with a
promise—"that it may go well with you and that you may enjoy
long life on the earth."*
—Ephesians 6:1-3

*Honor your father and your mother, as the Lord your God has com-
manded you, so that you may live long and that it may go well with
you in the land the Lord your God is giving you.*
—Deuteronomy 5:16

When families grow stronger as they "listen" to the Word, the
church will be reinforced; communities will be influenced; schools
will be better; society as a whole will be motivated in positive ways;
and business and industry may once again return the dusty plaque
to the wall that reads:

*So in everything, do to others what you would have them do to you,
for this sums up the Law and the Prophets.*
—Matthew 7:12

When I was growing up in the 20's and 30's the most conspicu-
ous public sign read: "Do unto others as you would have them do
unto you." This sign was displayed in the Sunday school room, the
schoolroom, in the bank, in the grocery and in the hardware store.
Wouldn't it be wonderful if our billboards and public vehicles
could once again display this motto? I believe that the world would
be a better place. Do you?
I challenge you to start in your home, your schoolroom, your
office. It won't be easy.
ARE YOU LISTENING?

TITHING MINT AND CUMMIN

My mother had a collection of mottoes, "a stitch in time saves nine," "a penny earned is a penny saved," "strike while the iron is hot," "putting the cart before the horse," "don't cross the bridge until you get to it," but the one that made a definite impression on me was, "a place for everything and everything in its place."

When things are out of place there is confusion. It is difficult to keep matters in proper perspective. This is true in tangible as well as intangible substances.

For some reason, the church seems to be the place where it is most difficult to keep everything in its proper aspect. Satan is ever present, attempting to disrupt and confuse. This is apparent in the area of dotting every "i" and crossing every "t" but leaving the most important matters undone.

The Pharisees were guilty of this and they were condemned by Jesus.

> Woe to you, teachers of the law and Pharisees, you hypocrites! You give a tenth of your spices—mint, dill and cummin. But you have neglected the more important matters of the law—justice, mercy and faithfulness.
>
> —Matthew 23:23

The Pharisees were self-righteous, holding their traditions for four centuries. They were legalistic, believing that one earned merit with God by scrupulously observing every technicality of law and tradition.

> Two men went up to the temple to pray, one a Pharisee and the other a tax collector. The Pharisee stood up and prayed about himself: "God, I thank you that I am not like other men—robbers, evildoers, adulterers—or even like this tax collector. I fast twice a week and give a tenth of all I get." But the tax collector stood at a distance. He would not even look up to heaven, but beat his breast and said, "God, have mercy on me, a sinner." I tell you that this man, rather than the other, went home justified before God.
>
> —Luke 18:10-14

The thinking of the lawyers and Pharisees was so out of tune with God's intentions that Jesus attacked them. We know the story of the woman taken in adultery recorded in the eighth chapter of John. These self-righteous people were in a hurry to stone the

111

woman but Jesus said, "If any one of you is without sin, let him be the first to throw a stone at her." Mercy was shown to her when Christ did not condemn her but told her to leave her life of sin.

This group took the law and changed it from an act of grace into a great burden. Jesus confronts them again saying,

> You hypocrites! Isaiah was right when he prophesied about you: "These people honor me with their lips, but their hearts are far from me. They worship me in vain; their teachings are but rules taught by men."
>
> —Matthew 15:7- 9

In our efforts to restore New Testament Christianity have we gone overboard in some areas and failed in others? Has our theology become one-sided—out of proportion? Have we failed to put things in their proper places?

In the second chapter of Titus, Paul gives a definition of sound doctrine. The older men must be temperate, worthy of respect, self-controlled, sound in faith, love and endurance. The older women must be reverent in manner of life, not slanderers, teaching what is good. They must also teach the younger women to be self-controlled and pure.

Love is the central theme of the Bible and is the greatest commandment recorded in Matthew 22:37-40. Jesus also said,

> My command is this: Love each other as I have loved you.
>
> —John 15:12

> For he who loves his fellowman has fulfilled the law. The Ten Commandments are summed up in this one rule: Love your neighbor as yourself.
>
> —Romans 13:10 (paraphrased)

What is love? First, it is unconditional—not judgmental or fault-finding but concerned, compassionate, merciful and forgiving. Love is also understanding and helpful, serving others' needs in times of illness and death. It is bearing one another's burdens.

> Carry each other's burdens, and in this way you will fulfill the law of Christ.
>
> —Galatians 6:2

Bearing the burdens of others does not include making decisions for them. Many trials and problems arise in life which must be handled by the people involved but in love we lend support and understanding. A statement by Colin Powell is very fitting: "You can't make someone else's choices. You shouldn't let someone make yours."

Many times well-meaning Christians, even church leaders, try to mend, patch things up and repair in areas beyond their jurisdiction. In their anxiety they forget that their responsibility is to encourage and support—caring and understanding. Jesus said that we are to carry's each other's burdens not make decisions for others.

> *Therefore, as God's chosen people, holy and dearly loved, clothe yourselves with compassion, kindness, humility, gentleness and patience. Bear with each other and forgive whatever grievances you may have against one another. Forgive as the Lord forgave you. And over all these virtues put on love, which binds them all together in perfect unity.*
>
> —Colossians 3:12-14

We ARE the product of our background and heritage. This influences our opinions and decisions, but it is imperative for us to weigh every opinion and decision in the light of the Scriptures. We must determine what God has said in spite of what we have heard from others in the past or in the present, making certain that what we are holding to is biblical.

> *He has showed you, O man, what is good. And what does the Lord require of you? To act justly and to love mercy and to walk humbly with your God.*
>
> —Micah 6:8

If we desire to be Christ-like, and I believe we do, we need to be filled with compassion, mercy and forgiveness. It isn't always easy, as we are human and not lovable or even likeable at times.

> *Praise be to the God and Father of our Lord Jesus Christ! In his great mercy he has given us new birth into a living hope through the resurrection of Jesus Christ from the dead.*
>
> —1 Peter 1:3

The Israelites were constantly disobedient and rebellious yet God was forgiving, gracious and compassionate as recorded in chapter 9 of Nehemiah. If God can show compassion and mercy and be forgiving can we afford to do less?

> *Praise the Lord, O my soul. . .who redeems your life from the pit and crowns you with love and compassion.*
>
> —Psalm 103:1, 4

A man with leprosy came to him and begged him on his knees, "If you are willing, you can make me clean." Filled with compassion, Jesus reached out his hand and touched the man. "I am willing," he said. "Be clean!"

—Mark 1:40, 41

Do you find it difficult to forgive? When we have been hurt and mistreated, intentionally or unintentionally, our human nature recoils and rebels, making the act of forgiveness arduous.

For if you forgive men when they sin against you, your heavenly Father will also forgive you. But if you do not forgive men their sins, your Father will not forgive your sins.

—Matthew 6:14, 15

Jesus said, "Father forgive them, for they do not know what they are doing."

—Luke 23:34

How could He say this while suffering physical pain beyond description—while enduring shame, reproach and unfairness? Would we be able to forgive in this situation?

If we claim to be without sin, we deceive ourselves and the truth is not in us. If we confess our sins, he is faithful and just and will forgive our sins and purify us from all unrighteousness. If we claim we have not sinned, we make him out to be a liar and his word has no place in our lives.

—1 John 1:8-10

God does not pigeonhole sins. There are no categories with Him, but we are inclined to classify sins. We feel that some things are worse than others. It is true there are sins which have more far-reaching effects and repercussions; nevertheless, God does not make any distinction.

In the first chapter of Romans we find a list of sins placed in the same category: greed, envy, murder, strife, deceit, malice, gossiping, arrogance and many others.

We must be watchful and aware lest we fall into the trap of tithing mint and cummin, but leaving undone the more important things.

FINDING PEARLS IN PAIN

Humanity at its worst—humanity at its best. What brings out the worst in us? What brings out the best?

Affluent times may bring out the worst in us, although this may seem to be a contradiction. When everything is plentiful—jobs, cessation of wars, good health and our lives on track—we may become complacent, self-satisfied, not feeling a need for anyone, even God. We become much like the rich man who said,

You have plenty of good things laid up for many years. Take life easy; eat, drink and be merry.
—Luke 12:19

But what did God say to him?

You fool! This very night your life will be demanded from you. Then who will get what you have prepared for yourself?
—Luke 12:20, 21

In the early 20's times were good, jobs were plentiful, low moral standards were the order of the day. It was the era of the Charleston, flappers and bathtub gin. In many homes the Bible was gathering dust on the shelf—people did not feel a dependency on God.

Then, suddenly, CRASH! The Great Depression. Jobs were lost, banks failed and the world came tumbling down. I was living in a small West Tennessee town at the time and many people took their lives, unable to face their losses. On the other hand, many came to their senses and returned to God. No longer able to fix things themselves, no longer self-sufficient, they turned to God as the only answer.

A righteous man may have many troubles, but the Lord delivers him from them all.
—Psalm 34:19

How are we going to find value in suffering and troubles? How do we discover pearls in pain? Many changes must take place—soul searching, self evaluation, throwing ourselves at the feet of the Savior and admitting our dependency on Him, seeking His mercy, His love and His grace.

My comfort in my suffering is this: Your promise preserves my life.
—Psalm 119:50

For our light and momentary troubles are achieving for us an eternal glory that far outweighs them all.
—2 Corinthians 4:17

God does not cause bad things to happen to us; rather, they are a test of faith and character. Suffering brings us to the refinery. Just as a refinery purifies and removes impurities and dross from metal or oil to produce a usable product, so our lives must be refined to make us whole and fit for His Kingdom.

When our lives become shattered from pain, afflictions, trials, tribulations and sorrow we must return to the Potter's wheel to be reshaped and molded again. We then enter the kiln that dries and fires, firmly setting us so that God can use us in His service and for others.

If we do not experience and endure extreme sorrow, trials, disappointments and despair we cannot qualify for the ecstasy of heaven. It would be impossible.

Look upon my affliction and my distress and take away all my sins.
—Psalm 25:18

Be joyful in hope, patient in affliction, faithful in prayer.
—Romans 12:12

Only when we drop to the depths of despair are we able to realize our dependency on God. Then as we allow God to help us, working through us, we can rise to the zenith of spirituality.

In order for us to help others with their burdens, sorrows, and troubles we have to experience these things. How can we comfort the broken-hearted if we have never had our hearts broken? How can we be compassionate over a friend's loss of a loved one unless we have lost a loved one?

Carry each other's burdens, and in this way you will fulfill the law of Christ.
—Galatians 6:2

When we become discouraged as we suffer physically and emotionally we need to keep in mind that we are being prepared to help others and so fulfill the law of Christ.

What does this have to do with pearls? Pearls are very beautiful and valuable jewels but they are hidden in shells until brought to the surface. The value of pain and suffering does not surface until we have weathered the storms of life—until we have been refined and rendered a more spiritual person, and not until we have been reshaped by the Master Potter. Then, and not until then, will the pearls emerge in all their beauty, and we will be prepared to enter the new Jerusalem where the streets are paved with gold and the twelve gates are each made of a single pearl (Revelation 21:21).

Praise to the God and Father of our Lord Jesus Christ, the Father of compassion and the God of all comfort, who comforts us in all our troubles, so that we can comfort those in any trouble with the comfort we ourselves have received from God.
—2 Corinthians 1:3, 4

THE MAJESTY, THE MAGNIFICENCE, THE MYSTERY

It is 7 A.M.—the sun is sleeping in but the sky is displaying an indescribable beauty. Soft, billowy clouds of mauve and soft pink against a background of blue hues are welcoming a new day in mid-October.

There is a gentle breeze moving the maple leaves while they miraculously change their colors. The only sound is a bird making a frantic call of some kind. Blue morning glories are hugging the light pole and others are entwined in the climbing rose bush—eager to greet the new day. It is the majesty, the magnificence and the mystery of God.

During a comprehensive study of the Bible for the past several years I'm amazed at the numerous times these words appear; MAJESTY, MAGNIFICENCE, MYSTERY. I want to share some of my findings with you.

The creation encompasses all three of the words. "In the beginning" is a mystery; man created in the image of God—physical but also spiritual—is magnificent, and majesty is found in nature and the heavens.

> *The heavens declare the glory of God; the skies proclaim the work of his hands.*
>
> —Psalm 19:1

> *There is no one like the God of Jeshurun [Israel], who rides on the heavens to help you and on the clouds in his majesty.*
> —Deuteronomy 33:26

Is there anyone who has not been awed by the story of the Red Sea? One of the most astounding scenes in the movie "The Ten Commandments" is the parting of the Red Sea. Later the miracles of the manna, quail and water from the rock can only be described as the majesty and magnificence of God.

Have you read the beautiful song of Moses and Miriam lately?

> *Your right hand, O Lord, was majestic in power. Your right hand, O Lord, shattered the enemy. In the greatness of your majesty you threw down those who opposed you.*
>
> —Exodus 15:6, 7

118

The power and majesty of God is seen in nature—sometimes in fierce, frightening ways and other times in calmness and serenity.

The voice of the Lord twists the oaks and strips the forests bare. And in his temple all cry, "Glory!"
—Psalm 29:9

O Lord my God, you are very great; you are clothed with splendor and majesty. He makes the clouds his chariot and rides on the wings of the wind. He makes winds his messengers, flames of fire his servants.
—Psalm 104:1, 3, 4

As we read Job's story we are inclined to focus on his suffering and his losses. We commend him for his patience and his unwillingness to denounce God, but this book is filled with the riches of God's majesty, magnificence and mystery. Take time out NOW to read again chapters 38 and 39.

God's voice thunders in marvelous ways; he does great things beyond our understanding. He says to the snow, "Fall on the earth," and to the rain shower, "Be a mighty downpour."
—Job 37:5, 6

When I was young I enjoyed good mystery stories—one of my favorite detectives was Charlie Chan. Usually the hidden events were revealed at the end. The Bible is filled with mysteries that will not be revealed and completely understood until we reach heaven. This fact together with His many promises heightens our anticipation and excitement for our eternal abode.

He reveals deep and hidden things; he knows what lies in darkness, and light dwells with him.
—Daniel 2:22

Mystery and majesty are found in the prophecies regarding the coming Messiah. Isaiah has many references to the coming of our Savior, Jesus the Christ. The fact that God would leave heaven and come to earth in the form of His only begotten Son, physical and yet divine is a mystery too wonderful for the human mind to comprehend.

119

*in the future he will honor Galilee of the Gentiles, by the way of the
sea, along the Jordan. For to us a child is born, to us a son is given,
and the government will be on his shoulders. And he will be called
Wonderful Counselor, Mighty God, Everlasting Father, Prince of
Peace.*

—Isaiah 9:1, 6

*Surely he took up our infirmities and carried our sorrows, yet we
considered him stricken by God, smitten by him, and afflicted. But
he was pierced for our transgressions, he was crushed for our iniqui-
ties; the punishment that brought us peace was upon him, and by his
wounds we are healed.*

—Isaiah 53:4, 5

For a complete picture of this beautiful and marvelous prophecy read the entire 53rd chapter of Isaiah. I don't believe that we read
this chapter often enough; yet it is our heritage and foretells our
adoption as children of God and co-heirs with our Elder Brother, Jesus.

*But you Bethlehem Ephrathah, though you are small among the
clans of Judah, out of you will come for me one who will be ruler
over Israel, whose origins are from of old, from ancient times [from
days of eternity]. Therefore Israel will be abandoned until the time
when she who is in labor gives birth and the rest of his brothers return to join the Israelites. He will stand and shepherd his flock in the
strength of the Lord, in the majesty of the name of the Lord his God.
And they will live securely, for then his greatness will reach to the
ends of the earth. And he will be their peace.*

—Micah 5:2-5

The event of Christ's birth completely embodies our three "M"
words. Can we possibly imagine Mary's thoughts when the angel
came to her? She must have been fearful, mystified, and awe-struck,
yet she answered, "I am the Lord's servant, may it be with me as you
have said" (Luke 1:38).

Matthew 17 gives the account of the glorious transfiguration of
Christ. Here on a high mountain in the presence of Peter, James and
John God acknowledged Christ as His Son for the second time. The
first time was at the baptism of Jesus by John recorded in Mark 1:9-
11.

How do we view the Lord's Supper? Is it a tradition that is so
ingrained in our thinking that it has become a ritual lacking the

deep, spiritual meaning that should be experienced each and every time we commune? When Christ instituted the divine feast what were the disciples' thoughts? The full impact of true meaning was probably not evident until after the ascension. Do you feel the mystery and magnificence in this all-important symbol?

The crucifixion maybe the most difficult event to classify with majesty, magnificence and mystery, but with a closer look I see all three manifested. How could the death of one man change the course of human history and affect every human being? The crucifixion was intended to silence the man and His message—instead it resulted in the magnificent resurrection bringing eternal life to all who will accept Christ as their Savior. God sent His only Son clothed in humanity to earth. He lived a humble existence without pomp or fanfare and was willing to endure the shame and suffering of the cross to take away the sins of the whole world because He loved us, not because we are worthy. What could be more majestic? "The mystery of God is: Christ, in whom are hidden all the treasures of wisdom and knowledge" (Colossians 2:2b, 3).

Have you ever tried to visualize the scene in the tomb on resurrection day? It is impossible. It is the only event not witnessed by another human being—think about it. Joseph was present at the birth of Jesus; John baptized Him with others present; Peter, James and John were present at the transfiguration; an angry mob shouted at the crucifixion as the women wept. But the act that sealed Satan's doom and sealed our pardon was of such magnitude it could only involve God, the Holy Spirit, and Christ.

I like to think that some day in the eternal existence that God will allow us to view this all-encompassing event. Only when we are clothed with immortality will we be able to fathom the mystery, the majesty and the magnificence of our risen Savior.

O Lord, our Lord, how majestic is your name in all the earth! You have set your glory above the heavens.
—Psalm 8:1

Glorious and majestic are his deeds, and his righteousness endures forever.
—Psalm 111:3

PURSUIT OF PURPOSE

Words and their various meanings are fascinating to me. The sound of a word may denote harshness or softness, strength or weakness, active or passive, joy or sorrow.

What about the words, "pursuit" and "purpose"? In my mind, they denote action, power and strength. Pursue means to seek, track down, search, strive for, aspire to, persist. Purpose when used as a noun means intention, resolution, determination, goal, target, mission, something set up as an end to be attained.

In the beginning when God created the heavens and the earth, He had a purpose. In the first chapter of Genesis, verse 26, God said, "Let us make man in our image, in our likeness." What was God's purpose in doing this?

I don't have the answer but I have an opinion. He wanted children to be co-heirs with His only begotten Son. He wanted to fill heaven with his obedient children who would enjoy the glory and majesty of an eternal existence, forever praising His holy name.

God purposed (ordained) that all who accepted His Son as Savior, submitting their lives to Him, would have an everlasting abode with Him.

This is the plan determined for the whole world; this is the hand stretched out over all nations. For the Lord Almighty has purposed, and who can thwart him? His hand is stretched out, and who can turn it back?

—Isaiah 14:26, 27

God has a purpose for each of us. How do we know this?

The Lord will fulfill his purpose for me.

—Psalm 138:8

Have we found our purpose? If not, how do we find it?

In the early years of our lives our purposes may not be definitive—or final. There may be temporary purposes or goals—getting an education is an example. If we decide to marry we purpose to be a good wife and mother. We want our homes to be Christ-centered, our children brought up in the Lord's way as we admonish them to find their purpose.

It may become necessary for you to take care of an older relative or an abandoned child, either long term or temporarily. This happened to me. Six months after the death of my husband I had to become the caregiver for my aunt who was legally blind.

I'm ashamed to admit that for a time I was bitter and did not want to assume this responsibility; I even planned to place her in a nursing home but at the last minute I couldn't go through with this arrangement. I took her into my home and she lived fourteen months. She was so appreciative that I felt guilty about my attitude.

After my aunt's death I realized that my purpose for those months was to make her last days pleasant and carefree. Now I'm glad that my conscience bothered me to the point I was willing to care for her in my home with some outside help.

A quote from Steve Flatt may help in similar situations:

BELIEVE that you can; DECIDE that you will; CHANGE the way you THINK; ACT better than you feel.

There may come a time in your life that changes occur. You arrive at a crossroads wondering which road to take; a detour may be necessary, taking you in a different direction. You cannot make these decisions on your own. You must solicit God's help. He will help you to find your purpose if you allow it.

Satan has devised plans to hinder you. He plants the seeds of fear in your heart—fear of failure, fear of people resulting in lack of motivation. He also may cause you to have doubts as to your abilities to accomplish any useful purpose.

If you're uncertain of your capabilities, make a self-examination to determine your talents and your special qualities. Also be aware of your limitations.

The purposes of a man's heart are deep waters, but a man of understanding draws them out.
—Proverbs 20:5

In his heart a man plans his course, but the Lord determines his steps.
—Proverbs 16:9

Each person has unique talents. You may be the only one who can encourage a particular person. You may be the one to lighten another's burdens. Be a friend—a true friend is one who walks in

123

when everyone else walks out. You have something to give that no one else has to give; something to share that no one else can share.

When you discover your special talents and find the real purpose for your life you are serving God. Even a cup of cold water in the name of Christ is a good deed that will be rewarded (Matthew 10:42).

Don't allow Satan to discourage you but say with Paul, "I can do everything through him who gives me strength." God's women working in unison with their diverse qualities can be a powerful influence in His service.

God will help you find your purpose and will lead you to your greatest potential IF you let Him.

THE CONCLUSION OF THE WHOLE MATTER

Of making many books there is no end, and much study wearies the body. Now all has been heard; here is the conclusion of the matter: Fear God and keep his commandments, for this is the whole duty of man. For God will bring every deed into judgment, including every hidden thing, whether it is good or evil.
—Ecclesiastes 12:12-14

It is an art in knowing when to bring things to a conclusion, whether it is a visit to a sick friend, preaching a sermon or writing a book. You don't want to stay too long with someone who is sick causing him/her to feel worse, but you don't want to run in and out as if you don't have much time for them.

A sermon can be too brief, although this is not usually the case, but at some point it can become redundant and thereby ineffective.

A book can be so brief that there seems to be very little substance; on the other hand, a book may be so long that the reader becomes disinterested and may be tempted to put it down without finishing.

Do not be quick with your mouth, do not be hasty in your heart to utter anything before God. God is in heaven and you are on earth, so let your words be few. As a dream comes when there are many cares, so the speech of a fool when there are many words.
—Ecclesiastes 5:2, 3

I do not know if I have mastered the art of knowing when to end a book, but I believe it is time to draw the curtain and close the door. I have benefited from these reflections and I hope you have.

I am only an instrument in God's hands as He dictates the words through the scriptures and as He guides me to set forth His truth. My purpose has been to fan the flame of desire within you as well as myself to be more dedicated as a Christian and more excited to serve Him in order to reach a deeper degree of spiritual maturity.

The end of a matter is better than its beginning.
—Ecclesiastes 7:8

POSTSCRIPT:
THE MORE YOU KNOW

At the end of certain programs on NBC the phrase "the more you know" rolls across the screen. Sometimes a person will encourage the viewing audience to read more on the subject just presented.

It is a fact that the more you know will broaden your horizons; the more you know will whet your appetite to know more; the more you know will make you a more interesting person; the more you know will make you a happier person; the more you know will make you a wiser person.

Do you have regrets in your life? Most of us do. We would like to undo some things and, on the other hand, we probably wish we had followed through on many things.

I would not want to live my life over but I do wish I had fertilized some of my pursuits. For instance, I loved French—my teacher was a native of France with black hair styled like a large bird's nest. She had piercing brown eyes and had a way of stimulating her students to appreciate her native language. At the end of two years in her class I could read anything in French. Speaking it was another matter, but I prided myself on being able to read *The Three Musketeers* in French before reading it in English. I failed to nurture this ability and have lost this acquired proficiency.

Certain things stand out in our minds which might not be noticed by others. One thing for me is the way a man in a certain congregation always began his prayer: "O Lord, we thank you for great music and good books." He never deviated from this beginning. This man was an invalid for many years but has now gone to his reward but I will never forget his love for good things, even though this might have been an unusual way to begin a prayer.

I pity the person who does not enjoy reading and does not have a collection of books. I know a few people who say they have never read a book to its conclusion and many young people today rely on Cliff's notes or other condensed versions. What a shame! So much is missed in the classics and other writings when only a synopsis is used.

There is one book that we must not read in bits and pieces—here a little, there a little. You know what I'm going to say, don't you? God's Holy Book, of course. Two or three Bible lessons a week with a sermon or two thrown in is not enough. You must read and study on your own with continuity and persistence. This will stimulate interest and desire and soon you will have an insatiable appetite for God's word. The events and the people will come alive as never before, plus the knowledge and understanding will be invaluable.

The fear of the Lord is the beginning of knowledge, but fools despise wisdom and discipline.
—Proverbs 1:7

Wise men store up knowledge, but the mouth of a fool invites ruin.
—Proverbs 10:14

A wise man has great power, and a man of knowledge increases strength.
—Proverbs 24:5

Read the first chapter of Luke for the beautiful song of Mary and the prophetic song of Zechariah as the Holy Spirit filled him with words concerning his son, John, after his birth.

And you, my child, will be called a prophet of the Most High; for you will go on before the Lord to prepare the way for him, to give his people the knowledge of salvation through the forgiveness of their sins, because of the tender mercy of our God.
—Luke 1:76-78

Do you watch the television game show, *Jeopardy*? It is a mind stimulant, interesting and entertaining. I am very selective in regard to television. I have decided that the devil is on the Board of Directors of the major networks—he may even be the chairman of the board. He at least has his dark angels working with the writers of the sitcoms and other shows filled with every immoral thing you can imagine.

I got off the track somewhat, didn't I? Back to JEOPARDY! From time to time one of the categories will be the Bible. Sometimes the contestants will leave it until last but other times it will be selected first. It is disappointing when the person fails to answer the simplest Bible question; on the other hand it is gratifying when a contestant answers all or most all questions on the Bible.

BUT just knowing facts without putting them into practice or some kind of use is of no value. In Paul's letter to the Colossians he gives thanks for their faith and says:

127

For this reason, since the day we heard about you, we have not stopped praying for you and asking God to fill you with the knowledge of his will through all spiritual wisdom and understanding. And we pray this in order that you may live a life worthy of the Lord and may please him in every way: bearing fruit in every good work, growing in the knowledge of God, being strengthened with all power according to his glorious might so that you may have great endurance and patience, and joyfully giving thanks to the Father, who has qualified you to share in the inheritance of the saints in the kingdom of light.

—Colossians 1:9-12

The craving for knowledge is a worthy desire and a pursuit of it brings many rewards, but the most important thirst for knowledge must be for God's word.

When Peter wrote his second letter he knew that his death was imminent, and therefore his message had a sense of urgency. In addition to warnings regarding the false teachers who were in error about the second coming of Christ, he stresses the importance of true spiritual knowledge.

His divine power has given us everything we need for life and godliness through our knowledge of him who called us by his own glory and goodness. Through these he has given us his very great and precious promises, so that through them you may participate in the divine nature and escape the corruption in the world caused by evil desires. For this very reason, make every effort to add to your faith goodness; and to goodness, knowledge; and to knowledge, self-control; and to self-control, perseverance; and to perseverance, godliness; and to godliness, brotherly kindness; and to brotherly kindness, love. For if you possess these qualities in increasing measure, they will keep you from being ineffective and unproductive in your knowledge of our Lord Jesus Christ.

—2 Peter 1:3-8

The more you know—THE MORE YOU KNOW.